HOLLY ANN GRIGSBY AND OTHER FEMALE KILLERS

REBECCA FALCON

Holly Ann Grigsby & Other Killers

Rebecca Falcon

Published by Trellis Publishing, 2021.

While every precaution has been taken in the preparation of this book, the publisher assumes no responsibility for errors or omissions, or for damages resulting from the use of the information contained herein.

HOLLY ANN GRIGSBY & OTHER KILLERS

First edition. July 1, 2021.

Copyright © 2021 Rebecca Falcon.

ISBN: 979-8224909407

Written by Rebecca Falcon.

Holly Ann Grigsby will go down in the annals of history not just for her murderous crimes but for her radical beliefs that she claims are "misunderstood." Grigsby and her ex-boyfriend David "Joey" Pederson went on a ten-day killing spree that spanned three states in 2011. Because of this, they're going to serve a sentence that will span the of their natural lives. According to the judicial record, there were four murder victims because of the couple's treacherous acts, but there are far more victims who have to suffer, mourn, and go on living without their loved ones in their arms as a direct result of their actions. We don't know much about Holly's childhood, or what kinds of things may have happened to her in her early years to influence her behavior. From a genetic and demographic background, there aren't very many white female serial killers at all. Holly is far from the only killer woman alive, there are a few, but how does she compare to other known female offenders?

Most of the women that have been charged with multiple murders have had a male accomplice, usually men that they were romantically involved with. It is not uncommon that partners take up beliefs or personality traits of the person with which they are involved, and this appears to be true for the serial killers in relationships as well. Such is the case with Holly Grigsby and her lover Joey Pederson. It's not clear who the leader was in these murder-fueled relationships, but there is little doubt that Holly was a willing participant in the pitiless slayings.

When we look at the other women who have committed violent crimes along with their boyfriends, we look at the relationship dynamic between the two. Who was the aggressor? Were both parties willing participants? Who's idea was it to start committing crimes in the first place? Let's begin by looking at some famous female serial killers.

In the 1960's in England, a couple named Myra Hindley and Ian Brady callously raped and killed five children. It was reported that Hindley and Brady, her boyfriend, would drive around in separate vehicles looking for young victims that suited their purposes. Once a perfect victim was found, Myra, a seemingly harmless woman, would lure the lone child or teen into her car. She would take the victim out to a remote area where Ian would attack without the possibility of witnesses. Myra was possibly more scrutinized for her role in the crimes than her boyfriend, because she partook in something that was far more sinister than simple violence, and was called "The Most Evil Woman in Britain" by some news outlets. After her arrest, she eventually claimed to be a reformed Catholic and argued that it was cruel to keep her imprisoned, but regardless of her claims, she still died while still behind bars in 2002.

Rosemary West, another infamous female murderer, started life with parents that were both mentally unstable and physically abusive. Sexual abuse was something she sustained all of her life which led to her having unusual and perverse opinions about sex. Rosemary was only 15 years of age when she met Fred West, a 27-year-old man who would eventually become her husband. By the age of 17, she had moved in with Fred, bore him a daughter, and cared for his two step-daughters., She was prostituting herself while Fred watched in their own home. Rosemary and Fred would find young girls and women to victimize together, and they were eventually found to be abusing their own children in the worst possible ways regularly. It was reported that Rosemary's own father was one of her frequent visitors, and he even had sex with his own granddaughter. Although Rosemary said she didn't help Fred abuse or kill any of the victims, the jury found her guilty of the murder of 10 people. Not including the families that they affected, it's believed that they had dozens of victims.

Karla Homolka, yet another female killer, helped her husband Paul Bernardo with his insatiable desire to rape and kill young women. She offered several female victims to him, including her own sister Tammy, which resulted in Tammy's death. Karla claimed that she was an unwilling party to the murders, yet video footage surfaced in trial of her happily torturing the victims. She eventually was sentenced to manslaughter (a far cry from what it could have been) and served 12 years for her role in the crimes. After being released from prison in 2005, Kara wed and had three children.

Statistically it's less likely that a woman will go on a murder spree without a man or accomplice to be the driving force, but when they do kill solo—there's usually a reason for it. Many female killers have had a caretaker role. This seems exactly opposite of the mentality one might expect for a serial killer, but it actually makes a lot of sense given their convenient access to potential victims. One of these known killers was Jan Toppan. She was a medical nurse during the turn of the century in Boston, and she admitted to killing dozens of patients because she found it arousing. After a mental evaluation she was deemed clinically insane and ultimately found not guilty.

Nursing home owner Amy Archer-Gilligan also finds herself among the ranks of these merry murderesses. Gilligan murdered at least five people, including her second husband, in order to cash in on his life insurance policy. Another caretaker, Kristen Gilbert, has been called "The Angel of Death" for the several murders she committed during her career by injecting patients with the drug epinephrine. Though she may have been responsible for the deaths or near-deaths of hundreds of people, she was found guilty on three accounts of murder and two accounts of attempted murder. She is serving four life sentences without the possibility of parole at the Federal Medical Center Carswell in Fort Worth, Texas.

In Mexico, Juana Barraza astoundingly killed around 49 elderly women in the 1990s. She would beat or strangle them until they died, and then proceed to rob them. It was said that Juana may have been killing some of her victims because she didn't want them to suffer, or because the trauma she endured as a youth led her to believe she was being merciful to her elderly victims.

Besides the quiet caretaker killers, there are also the black widowed women killer types, who have been found guilty of killing a string of husbands. One such vengeful woman, Nannie Doss, killed not only four husbands—she took the lives of one mother-in-law, her sister, her grandson, and her mother by poisoning them with arsenic. She joked during an interview with a news reporter saying that she was a "self-made widow."

In addition to the black-widow murderers and the angel of death killers, there are also the most rare category of female serial killers—those that seem to have no reason for it whatsoever. Aileen Wuornos is possibly the most infamous female serial killer of recent note. She admitted to killing seven men that she met either while prostituting or while hitching a ride because she claimed that they attempted to rape her, but no evidence of that was found. Aileen suffered an extremely abusive life, and she was most likely mentally ill. It was such a compelling and well known story that the 2003 movie *Monster* starring Charlize Theron was made about Aileen's experiences on the road. She was executed in 2002 for her crimes at the age of 46.

Despite the long list of women who have committed murder, men are far more likely to be the perpetrators of murder. The US Department of Justice stated in 2011 that men were the culprits of 89.5% of murders. A 2006 case report[1] about female serial killers concluded that "the most common motive identified was material gain or similar extrinsic gratification while the 'hedonistic' sadistic or sexual serial killer seems to be extremely rare in women. There is no consistent theory of serial killing by women, but psychopathic personality traits and abusive childhood experiences have consistently been observed." In other words, while men can kill for psychological or sexual gratification, women usually kill for some kind of reason.

Holly Ann Grigsby is a 31-year-old woman who, when she was younger, went on a short, yet horrific murder spree in 2011. As we have previously learned from the majority of female serial killers studied, she did not act alone in her vicious rampage. Holly performed her deeds

---

1.   https://www.ncbi.nlm.nih.gov/pubmed/16838388

alongside her boyfriend David "Joey" Pederson, an ex-convict six years her senior. She was in her early 20's when the killings began.

Holly was a former heroin addict who had been incarcerated off and on beginning in 2006 for crimes like identity theft and unauthorized use of a vehicle. She gave birth to her son while she was in prison, and she appeared to turn her life around. Shortly after the birth of her son, she was released on parole, and lived with her husband named Dan Larson and her son Danny in Southeast Portland.

She met Joey Pederson through a mutual friend in early 2011. Holly already held anti-Semitic and white supremacist beliefs, and she was wooed with Joey's stories of starting a white supremacist gang in the prison where he was last incarcerated. Joey was imprisoned for most of his life beginning at 16 years old for crimes ranging from assaulting a police officer to threatening judges. After his last stint, Joey became an amateur cage fighter, and Holly would often go and watch his matches. Sometimes she would even bring along her husband, encouraging him to befriend Joey.

Joey was able to seduce Holly away, luring her away from her family to be with him. This all happened within just a few months of meeting each other. He told her that he wanted to start a revolution, with a strong intent to kill Jewish people in particular. This idea really appealed to Holly, so she quit her job, stopped checking in with her parole officer, and left her husband and son to live with her newfound love. Weeks later, Holly would commit horrendous crimes along with Joey that would soon put an end to her freedom.

The crimes were committed alongside one of the most notorious roadtrips. The journey began when Joey and Holly went to visit Joey's estranged father, David "Red" Pederson, and stepmother DeeDee in Everett, Washington—because Joey wanted to end their lives. Joey had an older sister and a cousin that was adopted, and he believed that his father sometimes molested the sister and cousin, and that his stepmother had allowed it to happen.

After meeting, Joey and Holly and Red and DeeDee spent quality time together, and they took a trip to the shooting range, even though Joey wasn't allowed to own or operate firearms because of his felon status. To the average onlooker it would have seemed like they were trying to build bridges and form new relationships, but on September 26, 2011, Joey asked Red to drive he and Holly to the bus station, and killed Red by shooting him in the back of the head. Holly had to take the wheel of the truck to maintain control of the vehicle to keep them from crashing, and it was said that it took Red about half of an hour to die.

Eventually, Holly and Joey dumped Red's body somewhere, then took his truck back to the family house after looting Red of his weapons and credit cards. When they arrived at the home, the couple captured and bound DeeDee Pederson with duct tape, and Holly slashed her throat with a kitchen knife. It was reported that the first knife she used was too dull to cut DeeDee enough, so Holly grabbed a second knife to complete the slaying.

After they dispatched and disposed of Joey's parents, this was a turning point for the couple. They had experienced killing someone, and the murder-minded couple now had a new agenda. They could kill anyone they chose. Holly and Joey set off to begin a "revolution" against anyone who wasn't white or who practiced Judaism.

The couple took Red's Jeep back to Oregon and abandoned it, and asked their friends Corey Wyatt and Kimberly Scott Wyatt to drive them to Newport. It was there that they hitched a ride with 19-year-old Cody Faye Myers, a teen who was coming back from the Newport Jazz Festival. While riding with Cody, Joey and Holly tried to carjack him, but Cody, attempting to avoid violence, insisted that he would just drive them wherever they wanted to go. Joey shot the teen anyway, and Cody still tried to fight him off. Joey eventually shot the boy in the head to end his life so that they could take off with his car sans bystander on October 1, 2011.

Holly and Joey drove Cody's car to Eureka, CA, and eventually abandoned the vehicle there. After, they asked to hitch a ride with 53-year-old Reginald Alan Clark who was an African American man and a prime candidate for victimization. They shot and killed Reginald, and his body was later found in the backseat of his truck. Fueled by bloodlust, the couple then headed for Sacramento where they planned to terrorize Jewish organizations.

Joey and Holly's reign of murder finally ended when they were pulled over in Cody's car by a California Highway Patrol officer before they reached their intended destination. When Red and DeeDee's bodies had been discovered, an arrest warrant was issued for Joey and Holly, who were obviously on the run. The couple had been tracked to California by their stolen credit card use. Police also recovered bloody clothes, a knife, and stolen credit cards in a backpack left in a garbage can in Corvallis, Oregon on September 29th, 2011, that all contributed to the case that was piling up against Holly and Joey.

Holly planned on shooting at the officer who pulled them over because she wanted to go out in a hail of bullets, but Joey asked her to comply with the officer's commands. They were arrested on October 5, 2011.

During a five-hour long interview with the police, Holly admitted to the investigators that Cody wasn't the only person that they slayed. She revealed where to find Red's abandoned truck, and she explained that she was the one who cut DeeDee's throat, leaving her to bleed out and die. Joey nonchalantly told the police that he expected to be fingered as the person who killed Reginald because "the bullet from [his] gun is in his head."

It was immediately apparent from Holly and Joey's own admission that they were fueled by hate. Joey had several Nazi tattoos, and Holly had posted on her Facebook that "Every Jewish lie and every Jewish slander is a scar of honor on the chest of a warrior." Before her killing spree, she even referred to her young son as her "little Aryan warrior."

Holly and Joey were each charged with 14 accounts of murder for their spree, and their trials began in 2014. She admitted to racketeering, which meant that she was technically pleading guilty to all of the 14 crimes according to her plea deal. U.S. Attorney Jane Shoemaker explained to the court that she could prove that Holly was the one who cut DeeDee Pederson's throat, and that Holly used two knives to commit the act because the first knife was not sharp enough. Holly admitted to a California newspaper that she killed DeeDee because white supremacists like her believe that men shouldn't kill women, that only women should harm other women.

Senior Judge Ancer Haggerty asked Holly directly about her role in DeeDee's death, and Holly answered, "Yes, I aided in the commission." Judge Haggerty responded, "Did you stab her to death?" And Holly said, "No," backtracking her previous statements. DeeDee's two daughters and sisters sat in the packed courtroom, gasping at Holly's statements and sobbing.

Attorney Shoemaker said that, "[Cody] was killed because he would not give up his car and to eliminate him as a witness." Holly callously called Cody's murder a "casualty of war." Court documents revealed that they had killed him not just for his car, but because he had a Jewish-sounding name. Cody's sister and mother cried as they heard this story. Cody's sister posted about her brother on Facebook, saying, "He was reliable. He was faithful. And he was absolutely certain that he was called to confess what he believed to everyone who crossed his path." The chairman of the music department of Clackamas Community College, where Cody attended classes stated, "Cody was a humble, respectful and kind young man with a strong faith in Jesus Christ, which he shared with me soon after we met."

Attorney Shoemaker told the court that Holly referred to Reginald as a "negro degenerate" and admitted to killing him as well. According the the North Coast Journal, Reginald led a quiet life of hard work to scrape by. They say he was killed because he was black, when in fact, he was killed because he was there.

Holly and Joey's families were shocked about the killing spree. Holly explained in her plea contract that she was sorry for what she did but not for why she did it. She said, "Through October 20, 2011, we communicated with the media and other white supremacists about our mission, in hopes of sparking others to carry out the hoped-for revolution. In hindsight, however, I realize my actions were contrary to my ideology of making a better place for the white race and culture."

Holly was sentenced to life without parole in July 2014 when she was 27 years of age in the U.S. District Court in Portland. As a part of her plea deal, she won't be prosecuted in any other state or by federal authorities for these crimes. Attorney General Eric Holder decided not to pursue the death penalty for Holly even though she expected that sentence. She faced the families of her victims during her sentencing and said that the "desperation in [her] heart" caused by drug addiction made her do what she did. However, she said that any excuse she made would "make it feel like [she's] rationalizing [her] own insane behavior."

Perhaps the most shocking aspect of this case is that Holly has not abandoned her elitist belief system. She had this to say during her sentencing hearing: "My actions have further damaged the reputation of a movement misunderstood. I deeply regret this. Although I had nothing but the best of intentions, the bridge to Valhalla is not paved with good intentions, but with one's actions and heart."

Holly's mother Erlene Onofrichuk said, "This is not her. She's a good person. I know no one will believe it now. I just can't wrap my head all around this. And I'm terribly sorry, from the bottom of my heart and soul, I'm sorry for [Cody's] mom. And I know nothing I say matters, but I am so so sorry for all the families."

Joey was far less concerned about being forgiven or misunderstood. He claimed that the U.S. government is doing far worse than he ever did, by killing innocent civilians in Iraq with drone warfare. He said during his sentencing, "I can only laugh sardonically that I sit here, being sentenced for crimes for which the United States government has accused me. I offer no excuses because none are needed. [Our] western identity is being destroyed."

His own sister said to him while he was being sentenced, "Animals are treated more humanely going to slaughter than your victims were." Joey's mother Linda only stated, "All I have to say is that I love my son. I love him unconditionally."

DeeDee's daughter Lori Nemitz said to Holly, "How dare you go into my mother's home where she welcomed you like family. I hugged you for God's sake. I cannot imagine a person that would do that to an innocent woman who welcomes you as family." She went on to say that Holly's use of two dull knives to savagely cut DeeDee's throat was "beyond heinous, beyond cruel."

Holly Perez, Joey's sister, said during the sentencing that Holly will never be able to hold her own son again harming her own family with her deeds. She continued, "Separately, you and Joey are nothing but two cowards with skewed ideology."

Joey was given two life sentences without parole, so both of the killers will spend the rest of their lives in prison. Joey and Holly weren't the only ones to be charged with these heinous crimes. Corey and Kimberly Wyatt who helped out the killers after they murdered the Pedersons were sentenced for providing Joey, a felon, with a weapon.

The trials of Holly and Joey weren't as easy to prosecute as they originally seemed, however. Judge Haggerty rebuked the U.S. Attorney's Office during Joey's trial for misconduct that could have set both of the killers free. Joey and Holly's attorneys claimed that they didn't receive photos and documents from the U.S. Attorney's Office that they were owed while building their cases. It was later found that Oregon State Police Detective Dave Steele destroyed evidence and listened to confidential jailhouse phone calls made between Joey and his lawyers. He then lied to the court about his actions.

Judge Haggerty lambasted Detective Steele's conduct, saying that his means of keeping people from getting a fair trial could have allowed those guilty of heinous crimes to walk away from prison. He said, "It appears that because there was overwhelming evidence of guilt in this case, the government took a laissez faire approach to its obligations to provide discovery and protect defendants' Sixth Amendment rights. It is one thing not to review every piece of discovery and something else entirely to have reviewed so little that one does not notice numerous gaping holes in what should have been produced."

Despite Joey saying that he wasn't receiving a fair trial because of the missing or late evidence, he and Holly took the plea deal that put them away for the rest of their lives.

It's not clear what led Holly Grigsby to leave her husband and young boy to take up a killing spree with a known racist felon. Perhaps Joey's strongly-held values about white supremacy were more aligned to her desire to harm those who weren't "white" than her husband's values. Holly may also have been under the influence of drugs and may have been promised by Joey that he would locate additional drugs for her. Whatever the cause of this sad and senseless rampage, the killers will never be able to walk free again. With hate rising and fear-mongering becoming the norm, we may sadly see more racist female serial killers like Holly.

ANNA MARIE HAHN

SANDRA WINSTON

"Anna was flat broke. But when she saw a person walking down the street she would think that individual had HER money in their pocket. If she had to kill that person to get HER money, then she would take out her poison and say 'let's get this party started.'" - forensic psychologist Paula Orange

Anna Marie Hahn had a gambling habit.

She indulged her addiction at the horse races and bookie joints throughout Cincinnati in the 1930s. Anna wasn't very good at picking horses, losing time and again while accruing debt.

But it was an addiction had to be fed.

She needed a scheme, a way to acquire money to keep her compulsion satisfied.

Anna Marie Hahn was a clever woman. While walking through her neighborhood of elderly pensioners, the idea came to her like a bolt of lightning.

She would befriend these lonely and pathetic men. Cook them meals, keep them company.

Then she would kill them for profit.

EARLY LIFE

Anna was born Anna Marie Filser on July 7, 1906. She would be the youngest of twelve children born to a well-to-do Catholic family. Nothing in her childhood would suggest that she would eventually become a serial killer. She was never abused sexually or physically.

Nonetheless, she had suffered a few concussions during her childhood years during ice skating, biking and skiing adventures. These head injuries may have attributed to altering her personality as sometimes been the case of some serial killers. Anna also stated that she was a sickly child, suffering from blood poisoning, goiters, and scarlet fever. It is her belief that these instances led to "her mind changing that she could do the things that happened."

As a teen, she had given birth to a son named Oskar out of wedlock. The identity of the father has remained shrouded in mystery to this day although some claim a Viennese doctor had seduced Anna Marie.

She never revealed who the father was as he was a married man who wanted her to abort the child. Anna felt "just like a mountain was falling on top of her, not killing her but just smothering and crushing her."

The pregnancy brought shame to Anna's family. They sent pregnant seventeen-year-old to live with a sister in Holland until the baby was born.

She would return to Germany afterward and remain there for five years. The shame of being a single mom in a conservative, judgmental society would prove to be too much for Anna to bear.

"I could no longer stand those things that people were saying about my misfortune," Anna said. "I was afraid that my son would understand those things. These things were hurting my mother who was caring for my boy."

"Back in the day," Orange said. "Having a baby out of wedlock was the worst thing a woman could do in terms of family legacy. She had humiliated her entire family and was banished to another country. It certainly is an antiquated notion now, to shame a woman for having a child out of wedlock and it has become the norm. In Germany, however, this act was cause for ostracization."

Anna left Germany and arrived in the United States on February 12th, 1929. She had a step-uncle who lived in Cincinnati to whom she had written a year earlier. "I want to come to the United States," she wrote. "I'll repay you if you can lend me money for the trip. I will have little trouble finding work as a housekeeper. Please write back."

Her step-uncle, a seventy-four-year-old retired carpenter, was impressed with Anna's ability to provide for herself once she arrived. She did so well, in fact, that he became suspicious of how she acquired her money.

Oskar would stay behind in Germany with her parents while Anna would live with her now expatriated relatives Max and Anna Doeschel. Growing accustomed to the American way of life, she would meet another German immigrant named Philip Hahn at a dance. Philip was immediately smitten by the blonde and buxom Anna. The courtship did not last very long, a few weeks of dating was all the convincing Philip needed to ask Anna to marry him.

Anna agreed to marry him only on the condition that she be allowed to bring her son from Germany to live with them. Philip consented and the two were married three months after their first meeting on May 5th, 1930, in Buffalo, New York. Two months later, Anna would return to Germany and bring back Oskar who was now six years old. Philip would work as a telegrapher and do his best to now provide his new family.

Wanting a better life for her son, Anna convinced Philip that they should do more. The Depression was in full bloom but that did not stop Anna and Philip from starting their own restaurant and then a bakery. Both ventures would prove to be economic failures. The two soon became bankrupt and were forced to move in with a childhood friend of Anna's father.

Thus marked the continued humiliation of Anna. Branded as a whore by her own family, she was shunned and banished to America where she would suffer the indignity of becoming bankrupt.

GERMANS IN CINCINNATI

There was a sizable German population in Cincinnati and Anna was able to fit in and find friends. She settled in a community called Over The Rhine and she was welcomed with open arms.

She repaid some of these new "friends" by killing them.

"She had it all," author Diane Britt Franklin said. "She knew how to manipulate, steal, poison."

But what prompted her to turn to murder?

The friend of Anna's father had left his home to the Hahn's but they still had a mortgage to pay. Philip lost his job as a telegrapher, a victim of both technology and the Depression. The walls started to close in on the couple as creditors began making threats to take possession of her home.

Anna did not know what else to do.

So she turned to gambling.

Three years into her marriage, Anna was neck-deep in debt because of her gambling habit. She loved the racetracks but could never pick a winner. She would play horses at the Blade, a bookie joint in suburban Elmwood, Ohio then the gaming tables in Newport.

The addiction grew faster than her pocketbook would allow.

She needed money. Fast.

So she found a new way to "earn" money. Unbeknownst to her husband, Anna began plotting ways to pilfer money out of elderly German men who lived in Over the Rhine.

She developed a method typical of male serial killers in that she had a typical victim. Anna thought long and hard about what type of man she should target. The lonely. The old. The German, with whom she would be able to ingratiate herself to.

Anna found an apartment building in Cincinnati that was comprised mostly of older German men.

They were the perfect foil for Anna Hahn. A young and beautiful German woman who spoke their language, they easily fell prey to her charms.

"She went through apartment buildings," Franklin said. "She knocked on doors and asked for old men who were single."

"She developed a method of extracting money from wealthy old people," Orange said. "She would gain access into their homes by offering her services as a nurse. Then she would take their money."

Ernst Kohler was believed to be her first victim. Anna had befriended the lonely German man and he had willed his house to her.

Getting the sense that she was onto something, Anna began "befriending" more elderly men. The next victim was seventy-two-year-old Albert Parker who enlisted Anna's aid as a caretaker. Anna would borrow over $1,000 from Parker and signed an I.O.U for it. After Parker's death, the letter of debt "disappeared."

SETTING THE STAGE

Anna dressed her son in his Sunday's best before they went prospecting for victims. The little boy wore a brown suit with a beige shirt and a derby hat. Anna dressed conservatively, looking like a German mother taking her son out to Sunday School. She wore a gray jacket with a black silk blouse. But Anna made sure that her silver cross necklace stood prominently over her cleavage.

She then knocked on the apartment door of Jacob Wagner and put on her best smile.

Th door creaked open and the elderly German man peered out at them, saying nothing.

"Mr. Wagner," Anna said in a strong German accent. "I'm Anna Marie."

The old man's face brightened with good cheer. He had a young woman to help around the house with chores.

Little did he know that Anna would help herself to his bank account and personal belongings.

"She would take a nickel as easily as a dollar," Franklin said. "She would steal anything in sight."

Jacob Wagner was a retired gardener who only had a few thousand dollars in savings. He was targeted by Anna who would tell his neighbors that she was his niece. The old man became confused, responding back that he had "never heard of her."

"Neither Jacob nor the rest of the community fully realized what a psychopath Anna was," Orange said. "If you had something she wanted, whether it be money or material goods, she would do anything in her power to obtain it. If it meant killing you, so be it."

Anna knew that she only need to apply her feminine wiles on Wagner and he would be putty in her hands. She told the old man that she was an heiress to $15,000 from Germany. She wanted to pool their resources to buy a chicken farm but in the meantime would working around his apartment.

The seventy-eight-year-old Wagner would die on June 3rd, 1937, only months after hiring Anna. The day after the gardener's death, Anna would go to Wagner's bank and present a check that was made payable to her. The bank asked her about the death of Wagner, she had conceded that she had forged the check. Anna would not stop there. She would appear before a probate court with a will that left all of Wagner's property to her.

She had forged out a will but didn't realize that Wagner never developed the ability to write in English.

"I hereby make my last will and testament," Anna wrote on behalf of Wagner. "I am of sound mind and no influence. I have my money in the Fifth Third Union bank. I want my funeral expenses paid and all my bills. The rest I leave to my relative, Anna Hahn of 2970 Colerain Avenue, who will be the executor of my estate. I want no flowers and I do not want to be laid out. (Signed) Jacob Wagner."

She would steal his money to pay off her gambling debts. But the addiction would not go away.

Anna simply could not stop herself from gambling.

She would go to the racetracks up to four times a week and her losses once again began to accrue.

"Anna was very smart when it came to selecting the right victim and circumstance," Orange said. "But she was too stupid to realize that she wasn't very good at picking a good horse. She had a compulsive personality disorder. Anything that she saw had a positive benefit would be repeated over and over again. She became good at getting into the graces of older men and taking their money. So that became another addiction that she had to feed."

MORE LONELY OLD MEN

Anna would meet another elderly man in the mostly German neighborhood. His name was George Heis. She would arrive at his home and entertain the old man with her charm and gaiety, making drinks for him as he sat on his couch.

"Mr. Heis was a coal dealer that she met and befriended," Franklin said. "She got very friendly with him. He would take the money he would collect from his coal deliveries and give it to her."

George lived it up with Anna, drinking up the best bourbon and laughing it up in his living room.

He didn't know that Anna was counting the days when she would kill him.

One night, she would lace his drink with arsenic. He would remain paralyzed for the rest of his life.

"Arsenic loves to attack the endothelial cells," Orange said. "Those that line the blood vessels. When it attacks, those blood vessels begin to leak. Leakage of blood anywhere, particularly in that central nervous system, can cause symptoms such as paralysis."

Heis drank Anna's poisonous concoction and immediately began gasping in pain. He stood up and staggered around the room.

Anna simply watched as the old man's eyes bugged out as he tried to make it to the bathroom.

"She was heartless," Orange said. "She would watch the old man stagger in front of her, begging for help. Her only response would be to take a sip from her own drink as he collapsed to the ground and writhed in pain."

Anna would not stop with George Heis. She continued to poison men and the community was none the wiser.

"Yeah, all these people were dying in this close-knit community," Franklin said. "And no one was saying a word. Eventually, someone spoke up and said 'Hey, we're missing one.' And they reported it to police. The police didn't believe it. They didn't have any evidence to go on and they would just slough it off."

The coal company began to inquire with Anna for the money she owed Heis. She had to find a new benefactor and found one in Albert Palmer, a retired railroad watchman who had a small pension. She would meet Palmer at the Blade, the gambling joint where Anna frequented. Palmer became smitten with the youthful Anna who wrote the lonely old man love notes, calling him, "my dear, sweet Dady" (sic) and would sign her notes to him "with all my love and kisses, your Ann."

"I wrote like that," Anna said," because I regarded him like a father."

Anna would borrow money from Palmer which she used to pay off the coal company. Anna had provided company to Palmer and cooked him "homestyle German meals." Palmer was smitten by Anna but not so smitten that he didn't want his money back. Anna then took care of the debt owed to the old man by giving him a nice helping of poison in his mashed potatoes.

Palmer then became ill and died on March 27th, 1937.

CATCH ME IF YOU CAN

Anna was getting away with murder with no end in sight.

"Even today, you don't suspect a woman of being a serial killer," Franklin said. "They're not that many. But maybe there are a lot more than we think because they're hard to detect. They're very hard to detect. Who would suspect a nice German lady like Anna Marie Hahn of being a serial killer? You just would not believe it and the police didn't either."

Anna was able to avoid detection because of her ability to think rationally and plan out her attacks. Unlike some of her fellow serial killers, her murders were not done on the spur of the moment. They were cold and calculating with Anna waiting for exactly the right time to execute her victim.

That next victim would be sixty-seven-year-old George Gsellman.

Lonely and pathetic, he nonetheless jumped at the chance to have the young German beauty as his caretaker. She waited on him hand and foot, cooking his meals and cleaning up around the house. Her son would also quickly befriend the sickly Gsellman whom she was slowly poisoning with arsenic and croton oil.

Anna would use the croton oil in order to flush the arsenic out of the system. The oil would cause almost immediate vomiting and on its own could cause death if the victim is not properly re-hydrated.

Anna would take Gsellman for all that the old man had. He would eventually die alone in his room.

"Anna's appetite to get what she wanted had no limits," Orange said. "She wanted that money. Needed that money. That being said, she probably enjoyed the rush of taking someone's life. You don't do something like that for so long without a psychological payoff of some kind. Anna kept killing men not only for profit but because she liked it."

THE DEATH OF JOHANN OBENDORFER

"2150 Clifton Avenue was the home of Johann Obendorfer," Franklin said. "On street level is his little cobble shop that Anna Marie walked into one day because she had broken her heel while out shopping. He fell in love with her but she had other designs. Can you imagine how happy he must have been to have snared this beautiful woman? Little did he know that in two weeks he would be dead."

Obendorfer was the typical lonely widow that Anna would target. She entertained his affection for her by telling him that they should go to Colorado and live on a ranch.

Obendorfer agreed. Accompanied by her son Oskar, Anna would travel with the elderly Obendorfer to Colorado.

But they never bought a ranch together.

Within one day of their arrival in Denver, Obendorfer became deathly ill in his hotel room after Anna gave him some food. He was taken to Bethel Hospital and Anna registered him as being from

Chicago. "I didn't have any money," she said. "I didn't want to be responsible for any bill."

"By the time they got to Denver," Franklin said. "Mr. Obendorfer had gotten very, very sick. She had been poisoning him the whole trip."

She would deny knowing Obendorfer to the hospital staff. They inquired for some identification of the man and Anna leaned over her benefactor on his death bed.

"Old man," Anna said. "Tell these people your name. Tell them who you are."

Obendorfer could not even manage a whisper, he was so weak.

"I don't know who he is," Anna said, throwing her hands in the air. "He's just an old German that I met on the train."

Anna then left the hospital and felt that she wanted more out of the trip that what she was stealing from Oberdorfer. Prepping to leave town, she had one more heist in mind.

"The hotel owner had rooms right behind the registration desk," Franklin said. "One day Anna Marie walked right into one of those private rooms. She saw two diamond earrings on the dresser and stole them. When the hotel owner realized they were missing she filed a complaint with the police in Colorado Springs. By that time Anna Marie and her son had left town and left poor Mr. Obendorfer on a slab in the morgue."

An autopsy would reveal high levels of arsenic in Obendorfer's body.

While Anna was away in Colorado Springs, the police in Cincinnati had finally become suspicious of Anna. They searched her house and found some incriminating evidence.

The police would search through one of her purses and find a salt shaker with enough arsenic inside to kill off all the inhabitants of a small town. They also found a bottle of croton oil that was marked with the words "poison." They found a bottle which contained more than seventy grams of arsenic lodged between the rafters between the cellar and the first floor.

Upon returning home, Anna would be confronted by the police. They would interrogate her about the poison and Anna would deny ownership of the contents but want it back nonetheless.

The police chief at the time, a man named Hayes thought that his intimidating questions would force Anna to crack under pressure.

"There are an awful lot of men dying around you, Mrs. Hahn."

"I love to make old people comfy," Anna said. "It isn't my fault that all these old men are dying. I know it is very peculiar, but why pick on me, Chief?"

"We searched your place, Mrs. Hahn," Hayes said. "We found enough poison to kill half of Cincinnati."

"I have been like an angel of mercy to them. The last thing that would ever enter my head would be to harm those dear old men."

TIGHTENING THE NOOSE

Anna would visit a physician named Dr. Vos whose office was in a building Annie owned and occupied. The doctor would soon discover that many of his blank prescription forms were missing. Anna's husband Philip would come forward with a bottle of poison and inform police that Anna had, in fact, stolen the prescription forms. She would forge the doctor's signature and order the poisons from the local pharmacist.

"She would send our twelve-year-old son, Oskar, to get the prescriptions. One pharmacist refused to fill the prescription because of the boy's age."

Philip then told police that Anna had tried twice to insure his life for $25,000 but he had refused to sign off. After his refusal, Philip began to become ill with the same symptoms as some of Anna's previous victims.

Philip's mother demanded that she take her son to the hospital where it was revealed that he was being poisoned. He recovered but never spoke to his wife again.

With the evidence provided by Philip the police now had enough to arrest Anna Marie Hahn.

On August 10th, 1937, Anna would be placed behind bars.

"She got too cocky," Orange said. "She would leave behind too many clues, in particular with Obendorfer. She forgot to cover her trail and the police eventually got her on their radar. The irony was that the predator, Anna, now became the prey of the police as they spent months gathering evidence on her."

Anna would plead not guilty to the charges of murdering Gsellman. She claimed that she didn't know the man. But a friend of Gsellman told the police that they had witnessed Anna visiting the old man the night before he died.

The investigation grew in scope as the deaths of five other old men and another couple had all died without warning but with one thing in common.

They all were friends of Anna Marie.

THE TRIAL AND EXECUTION

"It took me a long, long time to find that it is wrong to be good to people," Anna said to a reporter outside her trial. "This doesn't mean I am going to be hateful from now on because that is against my nature. They can take a human's body, but they can't take their soul because that will go where there is justice."

When her case went to trial, it shocked a nation that had never seen a female serial killer before.

During the trial, newspaper reporters described Anna as "poker-faced, blonde German woman who at no time displayed any appearance of resentment or shock at anything that has been said."

The prosecutor in the case spared Anna no mercy.

"In the four corners of this courtroom are four dead men," he bellowed. "These men are pointing their bony fingers at this woman as they say, 'That woman poisoned me. She made me die in agony. She made me suffer the tortures of the damned. Let my death not be in vain."

The defense attorney argued back that the evidence against Anna was circumstantial and that she was a "victim of a cruel sequence of coincidence."

"What was shocking to everyone," Franklin said. "Was that the jury returned a verdict of guilty without mercy."

The jury would be comprised of eleven women and one man. The prosecuting attorney felt that if the jury was comprised of a male majority they would see Anna as a sympathetic figure. So they stacked it in favor of females.

The guilty verdict meant that Anna would be the first woman in Ohio history to be sentenced to death in the electric chair.

Anna still had enough charm and wit to play on the sympathy of people.

"The judge cried," Franklin said. "Because he had to sentence Anna Marie to death. He had no choice."

"At the end of the day, Anna proved to be like most every other serial killer," Orange said. "She thought that everyone else was beneath her in terms of intelligence. They don't think they can be caught and the vastly underestimate the scope and IQ level of the people around them which include the police. Anna thought she was more cunning that everyone around her. For awhile, she was. Then the noose tightened around her neck and she had nowhere to go."

The night before her execution, Anna would sit down and write out a twenty-page confession of all of her murders. She tearfully described every detail in the small journal, addressing it to "Dear Lord."

"On one hand, you can look at her confessional as a letter begging for forgiveness," Orange said. "But women like Anna aren't remorseful without a payoff. Cold and heartless, she wanted to remain in control until her final breath. Her confessional letter was yet another attempt at control. She wanted to be in charge until the very end."

"I do not show my feelings," Anna wrote. "My troubles in life, starting when I had my baby, had taught me how to control my feelings...I don't know what made me do it. All that I can say is that my troubles were so big that it must have turned my mind. I do not try to excuse myself or my actions. They were not me at all...It all seems like a horrible dream...I wanted to cry out that they were trying the other Anna Hahn and not this one sitting in the courtroom...Maybe it would have been different if I had only told my lawyers the truth. My lawyers fought so hard for me. But that is all over now...I do not fear my end and my last concern is only for my boy. I have written this confession with the full knowledge that death is near and I only ask one favor and that is that my son should not be judged for the wrongs that his mother may have done."

The sale of Anna's confession to the newspapers allowed Anna's attorneys to take care of Oskar's future. They moved him away from Cincinnati and had him placed under a new name. Her husband Philip would remarry shortly after the trial.

There are competing reports of how Anna behaved as she waited to be executed. Some reports describe her as pleading to see her son for one last time. Others describe her as mocking that report, sarcastically asking "do I look like someone who is distraught?"

Nonetheless, before being executed Anna pleaded for mercy. She had reached out to Ohio Governor Daley to grant a stay of execution.

"This was one of the most difficult decisions I've ever had to make," Governor Davey said. "Something inside me sort of rebelled against the idea of allowing a woman to go to the chair but the crimes committed by Hahn were so cold-blooded, so deliberately planned and executed that I have no choice but to permit the decision of the court to stand.

I feel sorry for her son, Oscar, but his mother has bequeathed him nothing to be proud of."

Anna would be sent to the electric chair on December 7th, 1938 at the Ohio Penitentiary in Colombus, Ohio. She refused to see her husband and son on the last night of her life but allowed reporters covering her trial a farewell party. Several of the newsmen entered Anna's cell. She had fruit punch and cake prepared for them.

"You gave me a 'good show' at my trial, boys," Anna said. "The least I could do was to throw a bash for you. I guess I'm not much like a 'beautiful blonde' now, huh? Well, give me a good write-up when it's all over."

THE ELECTRIC CHAIR

"Don't do this to me!" Anna screamed at the prison attendants who began strapping the electric belts to her leg. She writhed against the grip of the guards as they held her down, strapping her to the chair.

Anna screamed in mercy. A priest entered the room just as the black death mask was placed over her head. Her screams and pleas became inaudible.

"Our Father, who are in heaven," the priest said.

Anna could be heard repeating the prayer until the execution flipped the switched as the heavy jolts of electricity crackled through her body.

She screamed for mercy then continued the Lord's Prayer.

"But deliver us-"

Those were her final words.

It took two and a half minutes to kill Anna Marie Hahn on the electric chair.

"Did she protest her innocence to the last?" a news reporter asked her attorney, Joseph Hoodin.

"I won't comment on that," Hoodin said.

"But did she admit her guilt?"

"I understood the question," Hoodin said. "And I still won't comment."

Anna would be buried at the Mount Calvary Cemetery in Cincinnati, Ohio.

BLONDE BUTCHER : The True Story of Ruth Judd

ERIN SPENCER

In 1931, Winnie Ruth Judd killed two of her best friends then cut one of them into pieces. She packed their remains inside two storage trunks and boarded a train for Los Angeles with the dead bodies as "luggage".

The media circus surrounding her crime was a parallel of the O.J. Simpson case in the mid-1990s. Reporters and readers alike were hungry for every sordid detail. Ruth, as she was known to her friends, would be tried and sentenced for execution until being declared mentally incompetent. She would later be remanded to the care of the Arizona State mental hospital where she would "escape" over seven times. During her last escape, she would journey to northern California where she would adopt an alias and avoid detection for over six years before her recapture.

CHAPTER ONE – EARLY LIFE

Winnie Judd was born Winnie Ruth McKinnell on January 29th, 1905. Born in Oxford, Indiana, her family soon moved from town to town as her father preached in different Methodist churches.

She suffered from tuberculosis as a child and was sent to an Arizona sanitarium for care. It was there that the seventeen year old would meet a thirty-seven year old physician named William Judd. They two would marry and Ruth would accompany him to Mexico where he was employed as a medic for American silver miners.

William, a World War I veteran, became a morphine addict in trying to cope with his injuries. The addiction soon seeped into his business life and he began having trouble holding down a job. The couple returned to the United States and began moving from city to city. The marriage was not a happy one as Ruth could not produce children and had repeated bouts with tuberculosis while William continued to struggle with his morphine addiction.

By 1930, the couple had a "needle separation", living apart but still remaining on talking terms. Winnie who had usually been called by her middle name, Ruth, had moved to Phoenix, Arizona where she hoped the drier climate would help with her tuberculosis. She had found work as a nanny to children with the Leigh Ford family, who were well-to-do. Upon her arrival in Phoenix, she met John "Happy Jack" Halloran, a successful businessman.

Halloran was married but was known for having open affairs.

John Halloran was nicknamed "Happy Jack" by the press when they got wind of his philandering ways. He was the co-founder of Halloran Bennett Lumber Company. A jowly man with a jovial personality, he used his wealth and status to procure young "party girls" despite the fact that he was married.

The two met while Ruth worked as a nanny for the Leigh Ford family. Jack lived next door with his wife and spotted the frail but pretty Ruth sitting on the Ford's front porch. He engaged the young woman in conversation and found out that her husband was away at a rehab center fighting another bout against his morphine addiction. Ruth confided to Jack that she was lonely and the opportunistic philanderer made his move.

They affair began on Christmas Eve of 1930 up until the night she murdered Anne and Sammy who were also involved with Jack.

Winnie would quit her job with the Ford family and obtain work as a medical secretary at the Grunow Medical Clinic in Phoenix.

It is here where she would befriend Agnes "Anne" Leroi, an x-ray technician and her roommate Hedvig "Sammy" Samuelson.

The two women had moved to Phoenix from Alaska as they wanted a better climate after Sammy had contracted tuberculosis.

The trio would have a tumultuous friendship that hinted of a love triangle between Annie, Ruth and Jack as well as a hints of homosexuality.

CHAPTER TWO – A TRIANGLE OF LUST

Ruth become close with Annie and Sammy, often having sleepovers at their bungalow. The two women soon become friends with Jack who, being the philanderer that he was, quickly indulged in relations with Annie.

This didn't sit well with Ruth who mistakenly believed that Jack loved her.

On October 16th, 1931, neighbors heard screaming coming from the bungalow. But the yelling stopped as quickly as it started and no one reported the fracas.

"I had introduced Jack to a girl they (Annie/Sammy) objected to," Winnie said in a jailhouse interview. "That is what the quarrel was over. He (Halloran) was a friend of my husband but he was trying to kiss my behind my husband's back. And I loved my husband very much."

Ruth had shot both women in a jealous fit with a .25 caliber handgun.

She then dismembered Sammy's body and put her head, torso, and lower legs into a shipping trunk while placing her thighs in a traveling suitcase. Annie's body was not dismembered, instead being stuffed into another shipping trunk.

The morning after, Ruth showed up late for work at the clinic while her co-workers wondered about the whereabouts of Annie. Later at the trial, some workers reported seeing Ruth as having a bandage on her left hand. Some remembered it being on her right. Others didn't remember it at all.

After her shift ended, Ruth called a moving van to retrieve a pair of large trunks and have them placed on a train for Los Angeles two days after the murders.

Ruth boarded the Golden State Limited passenger train at Phoenix's Union Station with both the trunk and suitcase which contained the bodies. She arrived in Los Angeles but her trunks immediately brought suspicion as porters saw the "stained fluid" coming from the trunks which was emitting a foul smell as well.

The porter, a man named Arthur Anderson, confronted Ruth.

"Ma'am," the porter said. "There's something leaking out of your trunk."

"Is there?"

"You know, a lot of folks try to transport contraband into Los Angeles," the train agent continued. "I've seen it all. Had one big game hunter use his wife to transport a dead deer. You wouldn't do something like that would you?"

"God, no."

"Do you have the keys for the trunk?"

"Its in my car."

"Let's open it please."

"My car is just outside," Ruth said, heading out of the depot. "Just wait right here. I'll get my keys, unlock the trunk and then I'll see what's leaking."

Ruth's younger brother Burton arrived in his vehicle to pick her up. Burton, a USC college student, had no idea that Ruth just committed murder.

"Drive," Ruth commanded.

"Where's all your stuff?" Burton asked.

"Just drive, Burton! Don't ask any questions, just go."

The car sped away as Anderson stepped out of the depot. He had the presence of mind to memorize the license plate of the vehicle and immediately reported the incident to the Los Angeles Police Department.

The police arrived, picked the locks on each of the trunks and were shocked to discovered the dead bodies inside.

"I was the chief investigator of the case," retired Phoenix detective Charles Arnold said. "From the police department in Phoenix at the time it happened. At the time it happened, the Phoenix police department knew nothing of Ruth Judd. Never heard of her. Until our police chief, that morning, received a call about nine o'clock, received a call from the captain of homicide from Los Angeles. The chief had said that they had discovered these trunks with nude bodies in them at the depot."

The police traced the car to Ruth's brother but the woman herself had disappeared. Ruth had gone home with Burton then hid in a department store among other places.

CHAPTER THREE – THE TRUNK MURDERS

The horrific crime would send shock waves throughout the country. The press would refer to Winnie as "Tiger Woman", "Blonde Butcher", and finally the case became known simply as the "Trunk Murders."

On Monday, October 19th, 1931, the Phoenix police force entered the home of Agnes and Sammy. Neighbors and reporters were also on the premises, disturbing the crime scene. The next day, the landlord of the bungalow placed an advertisement in two newspapers informing the public that he would be doing tours of the crime scene for ten cents per person.

Because of the ad, hundreds of people came through the bungalow out of morbid curiosity.

With their forensic evidence now contaminated, police nonetheless believed that both Annie and Sammy were shot while asleep in their beds. Both of their mattresses were missing from the bungalow but one was later found in a vacant lot a few miles away with no blood on it. The other mattress remained missing.

Police would also find a letter that Ruth had written to her husband but never mailed. The letter described a multitude of sexual goings-on at the Phoenix bungalow. Ruth would detail straight, bisexual and homosexual trysts that the trio would engage in.

With his wife now a wanted woman, Dr. William Judd put forth a public appeal for his Ruth to turn herself in.

Winnie caught word of her wanted status and would meet with police on October 23rd in a Los Angeles funeral home.

Detective Arnold led the interrogation of Ruthie as they spoke to her in the funeral home.

"Mrs, Judd, don't you think if a doctor amputated these bodies he would have known where to cut them and had to cut four and five places to find the joint?" Arnold asked.

Ruth shifted in her seat. "Well, it wasn't the doctor. I'll tell you who it was. It was Jack Halloran. Jack helped."

"How did you get the mattress out to the vacant lot that the women were laying on when you shot them?"

"I never shot no woman on a mattress!"

"Oh, yea, Ruthie, you shot women on the mattress. Because we found a mattress out on a vacant lot where you set it afire. And it hadn't burned up. And that was where the two women were laying side by each on this mattress. Because the blood spots were in two different spots on the mattress. And now, matter of fact, these women were sound asleep when you shot them weren't they?"

"No, no, they were fighting me."

"Ruthie, they wasn't fighting you. How could they be fighting you when you had them both in the bed there and you shot them straight down through the bed because the gunshots went through the mattress? How do you account for that Ruthie?"

Ruthie sat and stared at the ground. "Well, Jack Halloran helped me do it. And he said I should do that in order to get rid of the bodies."

"I said a while ago you told us that a doctor did that. Now Ruthie your story is all wet," Arnold shifted forward in his seat, narrowing his eyes. "Let me tell you the story. You went out there with this gun to kill these women because this one woman had rejected your love isn't that right? You found them sound asleep and you had the key to the door so you went quietly in there to where they were sleeping and you shot them right through the bed there. Because on this mattress that you drug out to the vacant lot and tried to burn there's two spots of blood not one, not a big spot, not a little spot but two spots in the mattress where the hole went through. Ain't that right, Ruthie?"

Tears began to well in Ruth's eyes. She gulped hard.

"Then you cut them up back there in the bath tub, you want to make this story good about fighting so I said you shot yourself through the hand, didn't you?"

"No, no, no, I never had any gun."

"Oh yes, Ruthie, you had a gun. A little automatic. Same gun you shot the women with. I found the bullet under bathtub that you shot yourself through the hand with."

Ruth broke down and began to cry. "I'm not telling you anything. I'm not saying anything. I'm not talking to you again, ever!"

Upon her arrest, Ruth became the O.J. Simpson of her day. The people of the 1930s were unused to the immorality depicted in Judd's crime-murder, infidelity, lesbianism, and drug use. They was conjecture that Agnes "Anne" and Hedvig "Sammy" Samuelson were "lesbian party girls" who seduced Ruth into their lifestyle of debauchery and perversion along with their mutual boyfriend, Jack Halloran.

CHAPTER FOUR – SELF DEFENSE OR PRE-MEDIATION?

Ruth would describe her murders of Annie and Sammy as incidents of self-defense. She described getting into an altercation with Sammy initially, describing how Sammy took out a gun and threatened to blow her brains out. Ruth said that she fought back and they both struggled with the gun.

"I went into the kitchen to set down some tapioca dessert," Winnie recalled. "We were all in our pajamas. I went to put this down on the sink and Sammy came at me with a gun. She came through the breakfast room door."

"We quarreled violently," Winnie said. "About what I was going to tell about them and what they were going to tell my husband about me and so forth. That I had gone out with Jack. So the fact that it took place in the breakfast room door. I'm naturally left handed. I do many things with my left hand. I grabbed the gun with this hand (her left) and the shot went through there (her palm.)And I grabbed a bread knife on the table and I stabbed her twice in the (left) shoulder. And the knife bent, it was a bread knife, so I grabbed her hand like this (pulling her wrist back) and we both had our hands on the gun and one shot went through one of her fingers. I don't know which one. And one went through her chest. And one bullet jammed and caught me here (her left ring finger), at the top of the gun. And Ann came from behind. She got the ironing board from behind the water heater and came up behind me and hit me which caused us both to fall in the doorway. And we fought back and forth, wrestling for the gun in the door way, both of us on the floor. And the blood was all underneath the linoleum that was the only way it got there it was from the fight. She was not shot in bed like they say! It was in the doorway and the kitchen. It wasn't in the bedroom at all."

Ruth then called Jack to help dispose of the dead bodies.

"Jack cut up Sammy's body," Ruth said initially. "I couldn't do it."

She would later recant on that claim and state that Jack Halloran had called up a "Dr. Brown" and had him come over to cut up the bodies. She said that Halloran had some "dirt" on the doctor which coerced the physician to come over to the home and become complicit in the murder.

"Jack came with me," Ruth said. "And he picked Sammy up and carried her in (to the bed). And he got Doctor Brown. They took me home because I was hysterical."

Ruth would also claim later that she had gone to Anne and Sammy's home for a game of bridge. A fourth woman was there but had left. She testified that there was an argument about Halloran's introduction to another woman and that Annie and Sammy attacked her.

Ruth stated that Halloran came to the bungalow and after seeing the bodies, began plotting a way to "fix things". He went to the garage and came back with a "great, heavy trunk".

"Don't say a word to anyone," he warned her.

Halloran would be blamed for being an accomplice in the crime but after further research the decision not to prosecute him seemed to be the right one, particularly with the half-baked imagination of Ruth.

Her stories would remain inconsistent during her interrogation with Detective Arnold as well.

"So we interviewed her for about an hour," Arnold recalled. "And she'd tell us one story and we'd head her off on that. And then she'd sit there for a few minutes and she'd say well, 'That's right, but I'm gonna tell you the truth now!' And she'd tell us another story. We asked her 'where's the knife that you used to cut these women up with?' 'I never cut no women up!' 'Oh yes, yes you must have because there were in your trunk. Where's the knife?' 'I never had any knife.' 'Well who cut the women up?' 'Well, the doctor cut 'em up.' 'A doctor helped you cut them up?' 'No, a doctor cut them up. He was there. He's my friend.'

It was discovered during the investigation that Jack Halloran and Ruth were having an affair. Halloran himself became under suspicion for the killings and was indicted by a grand jury on December 30th, 1932.

Ruth would become the primary witness through a preliminary hearing which lasted three days.

"I am going to be hanged for something Jack Halloran is responsible for," Winnie said. *"I was convicted of murder, but I shot in self-defense[1]. Jack Halloran removed every bit of evidence. He is responsible for me going through all this. He is guilty of anything I am guilty of."*

Even Dr. Judd, the husband of Ruth, believed that the man with whom is wife cheated with was not capable of the crime.

"I know Jack Halloran," Dr. Judd said. "And it is very difficult for me to believe that Jack had anything to do with that."

Halloran did not bother to take the stand during his hearing. His attorney informed the court that Ruth's stories were the rantings of a crazy woman. He argued further that since Winnie claimed that she

---

1.   *https://en.wikipedia.org/wiki/Self-defense*

killed the two women in self-defense there was no crime committed and Halloran was guilty of nothing.

The judge agreed, freeing Halloran in the belief that putting him to trial would be "an idle gesture."

"Jack Halloran had no more to do with the case than I did," Detective Arnold said. "She tried to involve Jack Halloran to get him to finance her defense. And when she fell down on it well, naturally she told a story that Jack helped her cut up the bodies and so on. But she already told that a doctor that helped her but she never would give us the doctor's name."

The controversy surrounding the case did irreparable damage to Halloran's reputation. He would lose valuable business contacts and his social standing in the community. Six years later, he would die at suddenly at the age of fifty-two.

CHAPTER FIVE – A LETTER OF CONFESSION

In 1931, Ruth would write out her "true confession" letter below and deliver it to her attorney. This letter detailed both the events of the night of the murder and her thought processes. Her attorney, Howard Richardson, did not use the letter. He instead had it "buried" as he tried to get her off on an insanity plea.

"I am writing the absolute truth of this case, in full confidence, that you will use it as you see fit in your best judgment. Mr. Richardson, I have full confidence in you and trust you.

This is my first and only confession of the case of the homicide of Anne LeRoi and Hedvig Samuelson. Anne was used to the world, I truly was not. Jack was the only man I had gone with since my marriage. I was ashamed of things I had done. I could not openly compete with her, I was married and ashamed to. Day after day she lorded it over me, always smiling and fresh and sweet, well knowing she was hurting me with her taunts. Many evenings Anne would kiss Jack and caress him in our presence, then after he was gone gloat over not caring a thing for him but merely working him for money. It was not what Jack did but the continual taunts made by Anne which drove me beside myself . . . I could not stand taunts. I just went crazy. Those taunts kept me awake, I could not sleep. I cried. I even prayed. I wrote my parents to please come to me. I was losing my mind. Wild ideas kept me awake. I took sleeping sedatives, Luminal. I wrote Doctor my nerves were breaking. I couldn't eat. I couldn't sleep. I loved Anne still, but those taunts. I would take more medicine to quiet my nerves, cried to please get things off my mind, to sleep. Friday night I expected Jack. He did not come. I went to bed. Again I could not sleep. I got up, went over to Anne's house. My brain whirling. I was so excited I was panting for breath. Never did I have the slightest dream of hurting Sammy. She simply never entered my mind. Except to get Anne, stop those taunts so I could sleep. Nothing more did I think of. I took the gun and a knife. How I would do it I was not sure. But I had no intention of harming Sammy. Jack was as intimate with Sammy as Anne, but it was Anne's cruel taunts that haunted me.. . . I hid in the house next door. Anne and Sammy returned to the bedroom . . . After they retired, I went to the back door, laid the knife and my shoes outside the door, then crept in the unlocked front door . . . I sat down on the couch in the same dark room and soon fell to sleep clutching the gun. I awakened, Sammy had gone to the bathroom, that insane desire, that power lead me on, I started for Anne. My stomach was turning inside out really twitching, jumping out of me, outside not a tremor, but my stomach jumping like convulsions. I retreated, curled up and went to sleep again. I went back to sleep again. Oh again and again all night I don't know how many times. Sammy kept going to the bathroom, I started for that bedroom and retreated each time so exhausted I immediately went to sleep.

Morning! I heard the milk man. Sammy went to the bathroom again. I started to call her, tell her I was there. I really did. Then I began shaking inside and remembered what I had come to do so this time I crept past the bathroom door, shot Anne. It was a low shot. Sammy called, What fell, Anne? I was hurrying past the door Sammy came out demanded to know what was the matter. I was limp she completely took the gun from my hands. I was non-resistant. I said, Sammy, I am crazy. I have lost my mind give me that gun and I will blow my brains out right here in this door. She held the gun and said, you get out of here right this minute.

... I then picked up the knife and went back after her with the knife. As I grabbed for the gun, I stabbed her in the shoulder, the fight with Sammy in that breakfast room door; her own finger on the trigger when the shot went through her chest; our fight is all about as I have always related she shot me through the hand as I grabbed for the gun; the gun jammed; we fell to the floor, struggled and I finally got the gun and shot her and in my wild state I really do not remember where in the head. I pulled Sammy into the bathroom. I cleaned up the floor I pulled in the trunk from the garage. It was now about 6:30 or 7 a.m. . . I tugged and pulled and finally got Anne from the bed into the trunk. Now it doesn't sound possible but this all took about two hours. I left for the office . . . I had pulled the trunk with Anne's body into the living room. But the trunk was unlocked. Sammy was on the bathroom floor all day Saturday . . . This all happened in the morning. I stayed in my office . . . until 4 p.m. I then took the bag home with me with the gun, knife, pajamas and dress. I fed my cat and went back to the 2929 N. 2nd Street house at around 6 p.m. I really had nothing definite in my mind. No plans made. In fact except for an irresistible impulse to get Anne I had no other plans. I entered the house through the bathroom window getting a chair from next door to climb in. I pulled the trunk back into the hall tried to lift Sammy into it, but that was utterly impossible, I couldn't possibly lift her, she was too heavy her body was stiff. I then got two cheap knives from the kitchen and severed her body into portions I could lift. I was hours doing this and then inch by inch pulling the trunk back into the living room."

CHAPTER SIX – THE TRIAL

Three months after the bodies had been discovered, Judd's trial began. Ruth would not be tried for the murder of Sammy, only the murder of Agnes.

Richardson would be steadfast in his defense that Ruth was innocent by reason of insanity. He didn't allow her to take the stand. He kept the existence of Ruth's confessional letter to himself.

The case went to trial with the prosecutors taking aim at Ruth's self-defense alibi. They pointed out the fact that Ruth did not have a bullet wound in her hand when she showed up for work the day after and that her wound was, in fact, self-inflicted to confuse authorities. They further argued that Ruth killed the two women out of a jealous rage as she did not want her husband to find out about her affair with Jack Halloran.

The jurors agreed with the prosecution and found Ruth guilty of two counts of first-degree murder.

She was sentenced to death by hanging.

Ruth then behaved oddly in jail, screaming, yelling and making bizarre gestures. Because of her high-profile case, the Arizona governor gave her a special sanity hearing that took place only three days before her scheduled death-by-hanging.

This hearing became a spectacle for the media. Ruth put on a show, laughing inappropriately, clapping her hands, screaming obscenities at the jury and pulling out clumps of her hair. She then tried to take off her clothes and had to be restrained.

"She's been crazy all her life," Ruth's mother would testify during the hearing. "More or less."

"She comes from a long, lineage of crazy folk," Winnie's father, the Methodist preacher revealed. "Our family has been cursed with madness for over 125 years. It goes all the way back to Scotland."

The testimony worked and Ruth's death sentence was commuted to a life prison term. She was then sent to an Arizona state hospital for the criminally insane.

CHAPTER SEVEN – FUGITIVE ON THE RUN

Ruth would show a dramatic improvement in her mental stability during her stay at the hospital. She no longer displayed the same screaming fits or displays of anger. She fit in with the prison population and embrace the routine, all the while calculating ways to escape.

She left behind a "dummy" in her bed, made up of items around the sanitarium. Fooling the guards, she slipped out of the mental hospital only to be recaptured days later.

The prison guards had her on close watch upon her return but Ruth was determined.

She would escape a total of seven times. On one occasion, Ruth walked all the way from Phoenix to Yuma, Arizona, making her way along the Southern Pacific railroad tracks. These escapes would become a national joke because on slow news days reporters would remark, "maybe Winnie Ruth Judd will escape again."

These escapes would become a running gag among the more sensationalist newspapers. One magazine opened an article on Judd with the words : "When you read this story, the country's cleverest maniac may be at large again, perhaps walking down your street, or sitting next to you."

Ruth would return to her sanitarium after another escape in 1952. Inexplicably, she would be called to testify before a grand jury that was investigating state hospital conditions.

Ever the opportunist, Ruth would plot out another escape during her transport to the hearing. She was searched beforehand, however, and prison guards found a key hidden in her hair and a razor blade concealed beneath her tongue.

A year later, Ruth would have another sanity hearing. During this time she would spent a great deal of time trying to obtain her letter of confession back from her attorney Howard Robinson's widow to get this letter back. She had enough wherewithal to realize that if the letter would be made public it would be incriminating evidence against her insanity defense.

Richardson's widow did not comply but the letter would not be revealed until after Ruth's death.

CHAPTER EIGHT – THE GREAT ESCAPE

Ruth would stage her most successful escape on October 8ᵗʰ, 1963.

She coerced a friend to give her the key to the front door of the hospital and made her way out undetected in the middle of the night.

"About these seven escapes," Arnold said. "The woman, in my opinion, its just my opinion, but I've been around. This woman never escaped out there. She was turned loose every time she went away from that asylum. They wanted to get rid of her! And she wasn't getting seen very fast according to their opinion. And every time she went out of there she'd go out and try to get money from some of her old friends to leave town on and she couldn't get the money. Then somebody would see her and turn her in and then of course the hospital would have to go back and get her. And put her back in the hospital. And that was carried on there for a number of years as I say as everybody knows she's supposedly escaped from there seven times. Before she got enough money to leave town on (laughs)."

Ruth somehow made her way from the Arizona sanitariums to the San Francisco Bay Area where she took on the name of "Marian Lane."

She lived with the wealthy Nichols family, finding work as their live-in maid.

"One of the reasons I came here (to San Francisco) was to be near him (her husband)," Winnie said. "He's buried here in the Golden Gate National Military Cemetery. And when I go down there frequently, I put violets on his grave. I thought he was a wonderful person. He was ill and he was worth saving. And I worked very hard. Ms. Nickles knew I loved violets so she had a whole lot planted so I could pick them anytime and take them to his grave. Because I was buying violets and she said I'll plant the violets, she was that kind and good to me."

Her identity was eventually discovered and she was recaptured after six years of freedom. Ruth would hire attorney Melvin Belli to represent her and he fought her extradition to Arizona. Governor

Ronald Reagan, however, personally intervened, sending Ruth back to Arizona.

Ruth would be tried again and judged sane, thus ending her stays at sanitariums. She was sent to jail but only incarcerated for an additional two years.

Ruth would be paroled on December 22nd, 1971. Upon her release she moved to Stockton, California where she lived out the rest of her life without incident. In 1983, the state of Arizona gave her an "absolute discharge" which meant that she was no longer a parolee of the state.

Winnie Ruth Judd would die on October 23rd, 1998 at the age of ninety-three.

SPREE KILLER : THE TRUE STORY OF MICHELE ANDERSON

JESSE DIXON

A couple of misfits

Residents of the Spring Glen Mobile Home Park in Fall City, Washington, were familiar with Michele Anderson and Joseph McEnroe, who lived in Trailer 39 in 2006. The young couple frequently argued so loudly neighbours could hear them several homes down – according to Ryan Westberg, who lived nearby, Anderson yelled that McEnroe had "no job ... no money, you have no life!"

They were misfits, neighbours said – bizarre, even. The couple rarely ventured outside of their trailer, and when they did, they avoided eye contact with the neighbours and resisted any attempts at friendly interaction. Stranger still, minor things would send them into a rage – kids in the yard, a car in their parking spot, or a cat on their porch.

Corissa McGehe, who lived next door, said Anderson would often "yell and scream" before calming down and apologizing soon after. She was definitely in charge of the relationship, McGehe said. "(McEnroe) looked up to her, and she answered questions for him."

Although Anderson frequently claimed to be the "black sheep" of her family, her mother dropped by every few weeks with groceries for the couple, McGehe told the Seattle Times. Still, Anderson told people her family "mistreated" her, and that family members regularly took advantage of her.

"Money was always brought up," McGehe said, adding that Anderson was always saying that her parents had "quite a lot" of money. "It was always, 'we're really struggling, we're really poor.'"

Planning a future

The two had met in 2002, on an AOL chat group where fantasy roleplaying enthusiasts shared stories of swords and sorcery together. McEnroe made quite a few friends on the site, he told jurors in April 2015. He met several of them, including Anderson, in person.

"It wasn't a bad social life," he said. "(Anderson) came across very sweet, very cute. She sent me some old pictures. I sent her a camera. The pictures she sent showed her being pretty athletic."

McEnroe had been living in Glendale, Arizona, but after chatting with Anderson for six months, he put most of his belongings in the mail – sending them to Washington, where he planned to move to be with Anderson. He said that his initial impression of Anderson was a bit different than the way she had presented herself online.

"She described herself as Linda Hamilton in 'Terminator 2,' muscular but trim," McEnroe said. "She wasn't particularly muscular; she was kind of big. I was taken aback and surprised."

However, McEnroe didn't let Anderson's appearance change his mind about marrying her, eventually. He said he came to be with her "for love," not because of her size. At the time, McEnroe said she was "stringing another man along," and questioned his loyalty. He was able to prove himself to her, and the couple moved to the Spring Glen park in 2004.

According to the park's owner, the new tenants paid their rent on time – the full $390 each month. Anderson was working for Nintendo as a night security guard, and McEnroe had a position at Target.

Plans had apparently been underway for Anderson to start up an auto-painting company with her brother, Scott, called Pure Evil Customs. The company was founded in 2002, but Anderson was still paying the bills with other jobs – including filling in occasionally as a postal carrier on her mother's route in nearby Carnation.

The relationship between Anderson and McEnroe was strained due to the couple's tight finances, though, and in 2006, they left Spring Glen to move onto a property owned by Anderson's parents, near Carnation. McGehe, and many of the other residents of Spring Glen, weren't disappointed to be rid of the unstable, paranoid couple.

"They said numerous times that they feared for their lives," McGehe said. "They felt that they only had each other, that they could only trust each other. There was this paranoia about them."

Anderson, however, was not happy to be moving back to her parents' property. According to a former classmate, Jennifer Chandler, who last saw Anderson in 2005, the situation between Anderson and her family was "volatile." However, she knew Anderson had financial troubles and likely didn't have any other options.

This "volatile" situation was nothing new, though – Anderson had been complaining about her troubled family relationships since she was in high school.

Sweet and artistic

Duvall's Cedarcrest High School yearbook in 1997 presented Anderson, a senior, as a fairly active and artistic student. A member of the art club and the cross-country team, she was sweet and mostly befriended the "unpopular kids," Chandler said.

Her home life was a bit of an issue, according to Chandler. Anderson claimed her mother didn't understand her and treated her unkindly, and that her father routinely beat her. McEnroe backed up this claim, stating that Anderson frequently described her father as a "vicious person." She loved her brother, though, and Chandler noted that Anderson often spoke of Scott with affection.

"Scott was the only person she really trusted because they went through their abusive childhood together," Chandler explained.

Anderson's paranoia continued into adulthood. Chandler said she believed Anderson had received a diagnosis of severe anxiety, but due to her financial situation, was unable to take medication or see a therapist. Instead, she barricaded herself into her home and avoided people.

When Chandler visited Anderson in her "sparsely furnished" trailer in Spring Glen back in 2005, the windows were blocked with black material – because the neighbours were "out to get them," Chandler said. Anderson had told her the neighbours routinely spied on them, and had even tried to break in.

Chandler's impression of McEnroe was that he was "a little weird," repeatedly telling her about a "spirit guide" leading him to his destiny. McEnroe even told the jury about his spirit animal turned guardian angel, the crow, in April 2015 – as they were weighing whether or not to sentence him to the death penalty.

McEnroe also told Chandler he planned to marry Anderson and take her last name, which he claimed was because of a disagreement with his own family.

A long-time family friend, Mark Bennett, had previously owned a coffee shop with Anderson's surviving sister, Mary. According to Bennett, Anderson had been estranged from Mary and several other members of her family for some time.

"Mary had fears about her sister, not just that she was crazy, but based on her anti-social behavior," he said. "(Anderson) wouldn't return phone calls. Looking back, it seems something had been in the air a long time."

However, he maintains that the family never thought Anderson posed any real danger, adding that "if they had (felt endangered), they would have had her arrested a long time ago."

Strained situation.

McEnroe's family was growing concerned about McEnroe's new relationship.

He had last spoken to his mother in 2002, shortly after moving to Washington. He'd been upset with her for being evicted from an apartment he had leased for her, damaging his credit and, he said, preventing him from renting a new place in Seattle. He added that Anderson was angry with her, too. Then he hung up and never called his mother again.

Still, Sean Johnson described her son as a "good Christian," and spent the next five years searching for McEnroe with the help of her other two children. He'd never shown a violent side before, said Johnson's 18-year-old son, Ian Jones. He did, however, occasionally get in fights at school.

"(McEnroe helped me out when other kids picked on me," Jones said. "I talked funny when I was little, and he defended me. He told other kids to back off."

MdEnroe, who displayed a lisping speech impediment of his own, said he doesn't like hurting people – or even seeing anyone else in pain. Despite his classmates "treating (him) like trash," he never got in any serious confrontations while he was growing up.

"I'm not a confrontational person," he told jurors in April of 2015. "I don't like hurting people or fighting, or even arguing. I just don't."

Johnson had been quite protective of her oldest son, who was born in San Jose, California, with a serious blood disorder. His health problems led to persistent nosebleeds, and prevented McEnroe from getting involved with athletics. Instead, Johnson said he played "imaginative games," and got into Dungeons and Dragons quite heavily after he dropped out of high school. His teenage years and early 20s were spent working odd jobs, in an effort to provide for his mother and his younger half-siblings.

McEnroe's memories of his mother, according to what he told jurors at his trial in April 2015, are somewhat darker. He spoke of his mother bitterly, telling the jury that Johnson doesn't know how to "handle children," and even sarcastically mocked her religious beliefs.

"Mom was always searching for the truth," he said. "Truth can be an elusive thing."

According to McEnroe, his childhood was "unstable." He told jurors that he'd never known his father, and had been consistently mistreated by the "losers" his mother dated as he grew up. Jurors heard accounts of how one of these step-fathers had attempted to drown McEnroe in a bathtub, while another filled his mouth with shaving cream.

"The main grief I had was just alienation," McEnroe said, adding that he felt alienated from "everyone."

After a brief time in South Carolina, where McEnroe had gone to visit another woman he'd met online, he moved back to Arizona, where his family was living at the time. Then he met Anderson, and decided to be with her in Washington.

"He said he was planning on settling down with (Anderson) and having a baby within two years," Johnson said.

Desperate for a change

Anderson was sick of her family "stepping on her," according to documents submitted in court. If they didn't start showing her some respect by that Christmas Eve, December 24, 2007, she determined that she would just "kill them all." Police reports state that the slayings, the Carnation Massacre, was a "planned ambush and execution of the Anderson family."

Although Anderson and her brother, Scott, had once been close, the relationship between the two siblings grew strained when Scott married Erica Mantle. Anderson claimed she had lent her brother money years earlier and still hadn't been repaid – and with her parents, Wayne and Judy Anderson, pressuring her to start paying rent for the trailer she and McEnroe were living in on the family's property, money was a continued source of stress for Anderson and her boyfriend.

So, that Christmas, Anderson decided to take matters into her own hands. Over the summer, she and McEnroe had purchased guns from a pawn shop, and she planned to use them to threaten her family members into treating her with the respect she felt she deserved.

The Carnation Massacre

Christmas Eve, 2007. Armed with their handguns, Anderson, then 30, and McEnroe, then 29, drove the 200 yards from their mobile home to the white house where Wayne and Judy lived. Anderson's father Wayne was 60 years old and worked as an engineer with Boeing, and her mother, Judy, was a 61-year-old postal worker.

When McEnroe showed up, Judy was wrapping Christmas gifts for her grandchildren in a room at the back of the house – but when they heard a gunshot from the front room, she stopped what she was doing and ran out to see what had happened. McEnroe followed close behind.

Anderson had encountered her father in the front room. Her first shot had missed, so McEnroe stepped in and shot Wayne in the head. Watching her husband bleeding out on the floor, Judy began to scream – even after McEnroe shot her the first time. After she fell to the floor, McEnroe "apologized to her and shot her again, this time in the head," the court documents said.

Anderson's brother Scott, 32, and his wife Erica, 30, were due to arrive from Black Diamond to enjoy a festive holiday dinner – along with their two children, 5-year-old Olivia and 3-year-old Nathan. Mary was spending the evening with other family members.

Since Anderson didn't want her brother to see the bodies of their two parents, she and McEnroe began cleaning up the mess to prepare for Scott's arrival. The bodies of Anderson's parents were dragged to a shed just outside of the house, and the couple used blankets and towels to soak up the blood. Evidence was burned in a fire pit outside, as Anderson and McEnroe were intent on not getting caught.

When Scott arrived, Anderson confronted him and demanded he pay her the money she claimed he owed her. After she pulled out her gun, Scott charged her and tried to wrestle the weapon from her hand. Anderson shot him "at least twice," she thought, but possibly "as many as four times." She also shot Scott's wife Erica twice, as the wounded victim crawled over the couch and placed a call to 911.

Officials stated that a call was made from the house at 5:13 p.m. on Dec. 24, and lasted approximately 10 seconds. According to the King County sheriff's spokesman John Urquhart, the dispatcher told investigators that no one spoke into the phone, but there was "a lot of yelling in the background." However, the dispatcher said the noise sounded more like a regular Christmas party than "angry, heated arguing."

When the call disconnected, the dispatcher followed up with two more calls to the home, which Urquhart said went immediately to voice mail. By 5:19 p.m., two deputies were dispatched to investigate. When arrived at 5:45 p.m., they found the gate chained and locked, and didn't make contact with anyone at the residence – the dispatcher's log noted that the deputies reported they were "unable to gain access" to the property. However, police believed the victims were all dead before the deputies even arrived at the property.

"From everything I'm hearing, it wouldn't have made a difference," Urquhart said.

Before Erica had the chance to speak to the dispatcher, court documents explained, McEnroe snatched the cordless phone from her hand and removed the batteries. Then, he "allowed (Erica) to huddle with her children before he shot (her) in the head."

"McEnroe made sure the mention that he apologized to (Erica) after she pleaded with him not to shoot her, saying 'you don't have to do this,'" the court papers said. "McEnroe recalled how he looked at her and said, 'yes, we do.'"

After killing Erica, McEnroe turned his gun on Erica and Scott's daughter, 5-year-old Olivia Anderson. She was shot in the head "at very close range," according to the documents. The last survivor in the home, 3-year-old Nathan Anderson, was holding up the batteries McEnroe had pulled out of the phone. McEnroe said the child looked at him with "complete comprehension, as if he understood," but McEnroe went ahead and shot the boy in the head.

"I didn't want them to turn us in," McEnroe said, according to court documents.

When Judy didn't show up for work on Dec. 26 and was unreachable by phone, one of her co-workers went to the house to investigate. When she discovered the bodies in the living room, she called the police – who immediately began collecting extensive evidence to determine who was responsible for the gruesome killings.

Anderson and McEnroe's initial plan was to escape to Canada after claiming they had discovered the bodies, according to court documents. Upon returning to the crime scene, however, the couple was interviewed separately by deputies, and arrested on suspicion of homicide. According to court documents, they did not return to turn themselves in – but their motive for returning to the property is unclear, especially since the scene was "swarming" with crime scene investigators, deputies, and detectives.

"I don't know what brought them here, they arrived after we got here," Urquhart said. "They came to our attention and were arrested."

Neither Anderson or McEnroe asked law enforcement officials what was happening when they arrived at the property – even as helicopters were circling the skies above the home. They also never showed any concern for the safety of the family. According to police, both admitted to the killings shortly after they were arrested.

Groomed to kill

Attorneys for McEnroe repeatedly attempted to place the blame for the murders on Anderson, describing McEnroe as a man who deserves leniency – a vulnerable man who was manipulated and used by his girlfriend. McEnroe's lawyer William Prestia explained to the jury that Anderson preyed on McEnroe – "hooking" him and "grooming" him to help her kill her family.

"(McEnroe) is a man with a mental illness who committed a horrible crime," Prestia said during the opening statements of McEnroe's trial. "(McEnroe) is not one of the worst offenders, even though he committed, obviously, one of the worst of the worst crimes."

McEnroe backed up these claims, telling the jury that Anderson had convinced him to kill her entire family. He said he had loved them, noting that all six members of Anderson's family had been kind to him – while Anderson herself, he admitted in retrospect, had always treated him poorly.

"I did not do this because I wanted to, I did this because I was trying to protect (Anderson)," he said. "I was completely wrong. I know that's not a good excuse – I'm not trying to excuse myself, I'm trying to explain my actions."

In fact, McEnroe told jurors he was struggling with his own feelings of guilt and grief, trying to come to terms with the "disgusting" murders that he committed under Anderson's coercion.

"(I'm) mad at myself for what I took from these people ... their futures, their dreams, their lives," he said. "That's my portion of hell, knowing I have done this awful stuff."

Sentenced to death?

Initially, Anderson said she deserved to be executed for committing the six murders. Although she pleaded not guilty, which is routine in potential capital cases, Anderson confessed to reporters that she was guilty of the crimes and wanted the death penalty. If the jury agreed and went ahead with the sentence, Anderson would have been the first woman in Washington to face a potential execution.

"I need to be executed for everything that I've done," Anderson said in an interview with KOMO-TV in 2008. "Deciding that I want to die was the most difficult decision I've ever had to make, and I was able to make it without a second thought because I know what I've done and I want to take responsibility for it."

Anderson claimed that she had attempted to plead guilty to aggravated first-degree murder, but was unable to do so as the prosecuting attorney was still weighing the possibility of the death penalty.

"I'm a different kind of person," she told Seattle Times reporters in a phone interview in June 2008, from the King County Jail. "Life in prison is not enough punishment for me. I want the most severe punishment, which would be the death penalty. I think if I kill a bunch of people, I'm not sure I deserve to live. I want to waive my trial."

In May, Anderson underwent a full competency evaluation for the purpose of determining if she would be capable of assisting in her own defense, once the case went to trial. The information was included in a mitigation packet, submitted to the court with other evidence to persuade the prosecuting attorney to not seek the death penalty.

"There are no mitigating factors," Anderson said. "I've been evaluated by three doctors and I've been found competent. My lawyers are trying to force me into a life sentence because they're opposed to that."

Anderson prevented her lawyers from presenting this evidence to King County prosecutor Dan Satterberg, but after a new legal team was appointed to her in August, she apparently changed her mind. Anderson's lawyer Stephan Illa said she requested that Illa and the rest of the defense team fight to save her life, adding that Anderson's "mental health history" and family background would provide enough evidence for the jury to see that she was an "inappropriate candidate" for a death sentence.

Satterberg did not agree, however, and after ten months of debating whether or not to pursue the death penalty, he decided to pursue the "severe punishment" Anderson had initially requested. He said he came to the conclusion with feedback and input from law enforcement professionals, defense attorneys, and the surviving members of Anderson's family – as well as the "horrific details" that had been presented during the investigation.

"Given the magnitude of these alleged crimes, the slaying of three generations of a family, and particularly the slaying of two young children, I find that there are not sufficient reasons to keep the death penalty from being considered by the juries that will ultimately hear these matters," said Satterberg in a written statement provided to King County Superior Court.

"The death penalty is this state's ultimate punishment and is to be reserved for our most serious crimes. I believe this is one of those crimes."

In a July 2011 hearing, Anderson's lawyers told Superior Court Judge Jeffrey Ramsdell that Anderson was "highly emotional" and wouldn't be able to assist in her own defense – leading to a second evaluation of Anderson's mental competency. Western State Hospital deemed Anderson mentally fit to stand trial.

In 2013, Anderson's lawyer's submitted a request for Anderson to be provided with a television or radio, and to enjoy an additional hour outside of her jail cell each day. Since her arrest in 2007, Anderson had been primarily placed in administrative segregation – and had refused to speak to her attorneys or to a defense psychologist.

According to Anderson's lawyers, the additional external stimulation may have helped stabilize Anderson's mental health and prompted her to engage with her defense team, but Judge Jeffrey Ramsdell denied the request.

In April 2015, when the jury that convicted McEnroe chose not to give him the death penalty, prosecutors made the announcement that they would no longer seek the death penalty against Anderson. McEnroe's punishment, as determined by the jury, was six life sentences without the possibility of parole – the same sentence Anderson received from a separate jury the following year.

The sentence came after members of the jury heard heartbreaking testimonies from family members and friends who spoke on behalf of the victims of the Carnation Massacre. Still, Anderson showed little emotion during the hearing and her sentencing, and declined the opportunity to speak.

"Look at what you have done to your life, look at what you did to your family," said Anderson's sister Mary, as Anderson was being sentenced. "Your brother loved you so much."

The fallout

With a population of only 2,000 people, Carnation, Washington, is a quiet town full of secluded neighbourhoods – the kind of place where, according to a neighbour of the Anderson family, people "mostly keep to themselves." However, everyone knew Judy Anderson, who delivered mail down Carnation's main street.

"I pass her every day when I'm going to work," said Cherrie Provo, manager of the Ixtapa Mexican restaurant in Carnation. "She always seems pleasant. It's a horrible, sad thing."

People live in Carnation for the country lifestyle, with goats and ponies lazily grazing along even the town's main thoroughfares. After the massacre, residents were shocked that a mass murder like that could happen in such a peaceful community – where "you never hear anything but coyotes." In fact, many consider the slayings to be among the most heinous crimes in the history of King County.

Prosecutors hoped the sentencings, in 2015 and 2016, would help the family finally heal from the tragedy - both Anderson and McEnroe will die in prison. While she was relieved that the "agonizing testimony" and legal battle was over, Pam Mantle, whose daughter Erica and two grandchildren were killed in the massacre, said she worries the community will forget about the murders and the impact they had on the town.

For Mantle, though, "the pain of losing so many family members is never going to go away."

CHRISTA PIKE

CHRISTINE CARTER

Christa Gail Pike, born 10 March 1976, currently sits on Tennessee's death row for the murder of Colleen Slemmer, 19, on 12 January 1995. The murder occurred when Pike was 18 years old. Pike and her then-boyfriend Tadaryl Shipp who was 17 at the time of the murder were convicted of Slemmer's murder and conspiracy to commit murder. Another friend of the defendants and the victim, Shadolla Peterson, also 18 at the time, was convicted as an accessory after the fact and given six years' probation after turning informant. Pike was sentenced to death by electrocution in 1996 and, at the time, she had the distinction of being the youngest woman ever to be sentenced to death, in any state and only the second women given the death penalty in Tennessee.

Early Life

Pike's life reads like a primer for depraved murderers. As a small child, Pike did not enjoy a healthy and supportive bond with her mother, Carissa Hansen, a licensed nurse, allegedly because of her premature birth. Whereas thousands of children are born prematurely and do not resort to criminal behavior Pike's birth was presented as evidence of one possible origin of her poor and troubled behavior. Pike's maternal grandmother was verbally abusive and Pike was raised by her alcoholic and abusive paternal grandmother until the latter's death in 1988 when Pike was 12; after which Pike attempted suicide by overdosing. She was then shuttled back and forth between her divorced parents' homes. In 1989, Pike was kicked out of her father's house for the second and final time due to her unruliness and the alleged sexual abuse of her father's then-two-year old daughter with his second wife.

Prior to the murder, experts assert that there were myriad indications that Pike was seriously disturbed; however, nobody who may have suspected this sought help for the increasingly disobedient and incorrigible young lady. According to Pike's mother, she was problematic since the age of eight and the two of them had a contentious relationship due to Pike's fluctuating and troubling behavior. Her mother asserted that by age nine Pike was growing marijuana in pots at their home and had been permitted to have a live-in boyfriend at age 14. At one point—in an effort to improve their relationship—Hansen suggested that she and Pike smoke marijuana together. Hansen mistakenly believed that cultivating a friendship with her daughter would cultivate the necessary bond Pike had been lacking her entire life. At one point, one of her mother's boyfriends whipped Pike with a belt which prompted her to wield a butcher knife against him before he was subsequently arrested. Hansen also admitted that Pike had repeatedly lied to and stolen from her. In several interviews with Hansen throughout Pike's trial and seemingly endless appeals, she admitted repeatedly that she was a terrible mother and should have spent more time with her daughter.

Pike's aunt, Carrie Ross, provided insight into Pike's upbringing when she testified that she disallowed her own children from associating with Pike because she lived in a filthy house that had zero ground rules and that Pike was a pathological liar of whom she was somewhat afraid. She also admitted that there was a history of substance abuse in Pike's family. Ross also stated that on the few occasions that Pike actually visited her she behaved like a little girl and engaged in Barbie and dress-up play with her eleven-year-old cousin. Further, there were some allegations that Pike may have been sexually abused but these were neither confirmed nor denied.

Pike's father, Glenn Pike testified that he did, in fact, kick his daughter out of his house multiple times; the last time being in 1989 after the aforementioned allegations that Pike sexually abused her two-year old half-sister. He admitted that he had signed adoption papers for Pike prior to her 18th birthday and that during the times she resided with him she was manipulative, disobedient, and dishonest.

After dropping out of high school, Pike began Job Corps classes in computer programming. Job Corps is a government-based organization that provides occupational and vocational training to underprivileged and troubled teens. It was at the now-defunct Job Corps center in Knoxville where she met Shipp, Slemmer, and Peterson. While Job Corps seeks to promote prosocial behavior and foster a strong desire among its participants to learn a vocation and secure a more promising future than might have been previously the case, this program is also known to cultivate criminal activity, likely due to the association among its participants; many of whom already had problematic behavior.

Evidence of Premeditation

On 11 January 1995, the day before the actual homicide, Pike told friend and co-Job Corps student Kim Iloilo that she was planning to kill Slemmer because she "just felt mean that day." Iloilo discounted Pike's statement as nothing more than merely talk; however, the following evening at approximately 8:00 p.m. Iloilo witnessed Pike, Shipp, Peterson, and Slemmer leaving the Job Corps center. When Iloilo saw Pike, Shipp, and Peterson returning at approximately 10:15 p.m. without Slemmer she, again, thought nothing of it. Even when Pike visited Iloilo's dorm room at 11:00 p.m. that night and confessed to killing Slemmer—as well as showing Iloilo what Pike identified as a piece of Slemmer's skull—Iloilo still failed to tell anyone. Later, at Pike's trial, Iloilo testified that while Pike was iterating the events of the murder she was oddly smiling, singing, and dancing around the room. The following morning Iloilo asked Pike what she was going to do with the piece of skull. Pike nonchalantly replied that she had it in her pocket and was, in fact, eating breakfast with it.

Pike also told another student, Stephanie Wilson, a similar account the following day and proudly described the brown spots on her shoes as blood. Not unlike Iloilo, Wilson failed to immediately report anything.

The Crime Scene

On 13 January, officers from the University of Tennessee and Knoxville Police Departments were dispatched to greenhouses on the

University's agricultural campus in Tyson Park where a University grounds department employee reported finding, at approximately 8:05 a.m., what he assumed to be a dead animal. The gruesome discovery was a corpse that turned out to be Colleen Slemmer. She was naked from the waist up; her throat was cut; her head had been bludgeoned; and she had various cuts all over her arms, throat, and torso—including a pentagram that had been carved into her chest. Officer John Terry Johnson who testified at Pike's trial described Slemmer's body as so badly beaten that she was unrecognizable as a human being. He also stated that he thought he was looking at her face when, in reality, Slemmer was lying face-down in the dirt and debris where Pike, Shipp, and Peterson had left her.

There was additional evidence and testimony that the crime scene encompassed an area that measured 100 feet long by 60 feet wide; an astounding 6,000 square feet in area. Despite the area being muddy and wet there was ample evidence of a physical struggle with trampled bushes, a considerable amount of blood, body drag marks, and hand and knee prints. Thirty feet from Slemmer's body was a large pool of blood which suggested that Slemmer was attacked in one area and then dragged to where her body was later found. Slemmer's shirt and bra were also discovered at the crime scene, as well as a bloody rag that Pike admitted to tying over Slemmer's mouth at one point to keep her from screaming.

Disturbingly, University of Tennessee police officer Harold James Underwood, Jr., who was the officer assigned to secure the crime scene, testified at trial that Pike and a few other females came to the scene between four and five p.m. the day of the discovery and before Pike was even considered to be a suspect. Underwood stated that Pike had asked why the wooded area was marked off, who the victim was, and whether police had any leads as to who the suspect or suspects were. He particularly recalled Pike's odd behavior—moving around a lot while giggling amusedly—and that she wore a necklace in the shape of a pentagram. The following day, during briefing when informed that the victim had a pentagram carved into her chest, Underwood reported Pike's behavior and necklace to his supervisors.

Autopsy and Findings

During Slemmer's autopsy, the medical examiner, Dr. Sandra Elkins, had to identify the victim's body from dental records because her head was so bludgeoned that she was unrecognizable. After cleaning up Slemmer's body which was clad only in jeans, socks, and shoes, and covered with dirt and twigs, Dr. Elkins began cataloging Slemmer's wounds. Due to the sheer number of wounds on her back, arms, abdomen, and chest, and the fact that following department policy which stated that each individual wound be assigned a letter of the alphabet, when Dr. Elkins reached double letters she, instead, individually catalogued only the most serious wounds and that there were innumerable other superficial and defensive wounds. Among the most serious cuts was a six-inch gaping wound across Slemmer's throat that was deep enough to penetrate the fat and muscles in her neck as well as the aforementioned pentagram. Additional injuries included fresh bruising which Dr. Elkins asserted was consistent with crawling.

Cause of death was ultimately attributed to blunt force trauma to the head. Dr. Elkins surmised that Slemmer's head was hit with the asphalt at least four times—two to the left side, one over the right eye, and one to the nose—which collectively resulted in multiple and extensive skull fractures. One of these blows was to the left side of Slemmer's head—which, according to Dr. Elkins, occurred with the right side of the victim's head against a firm surface. This blow only fractured her skull but also imbedded a portion of Slemmer's skull into her head and contained black particles from the piece of asphalt determined to be the murder weapon.

Even more tragic was Dr. Elkins' findings that none of Slemmer's other wounds would have rendered her unconscious and evidence of active blood flow around the wounds and blood in her sinus cavity indicated that Slemmer was alive during the severe torture she suffered before being killed.

Arrest and Confession

The police quickly connected Pike to the homicide thanks to the piece of Slemmer's skull discovered in Pike's jacket pocket. Pike had left this jacket hanging on the back of a chair in Job Corps Orientation Specialist Robert A. Pollock's office on 13 January after meeting with him about a misplaced ID card. Pike's jacket remained in Pollock's office from 4:00 p.m. on 13 January until 7:30 a.m. on 17 January. After learning over the weekend that Pike was a suspect in Slemmer's murder investigation, Pollock immediately gave the jacket to William Hudson, the Job Corps' safety and security captain who turned it over to Knoxville Police Department Officer Arthur Bohanan. At trial, Bohanan would testify that he found a small piece of bone in one of the pockets and presented it to Dr. Murray Marks, a University of Tennessee forensic anthropologist who was reconstructing Slemmer's decapitated skull and the piece in Pike's jacket pocket fit perfectly into an area where a portion of her skull was missing at the time of the victim's discovery.

When confronted with this evidence and subsequently arrested, Pike waived her *Miranda* protections and confessed to the murder and permitted officers to search her dorm room where the blood-soaked jeans she wore the previous night were found. Additionally, Pike led officers to a trash can at a nearby Texaco station on Cumberland Avenue where she had disposed of Slemmer's ID and a pair of gloves Pike had been wearing at the time of the homicide.

Pike's transcribed confession was 46 pages long.

In it, Pike admitted that there was animosity between Slemmer and her because Pike was convinced that Slemmer was a rival for the affections of her boyfriend, Shipp, and that Slemmer was trying to get Pike kicked out of the Job Corps program so she could have Shipp for herself. Pike also claimed that she had awakened one night to find

Slemmer standing above her with a box cutter; however, there is no evidence of this allegation. Instead, Slemmer had repeatedly called her mother, May Martinez, to tell her she was afraid of Pike who she had awakened to find in her room and that she wanted to come home; to which Slemmer's mother said that she couldn't because she had signed a contract. Pike stated that she had only planned to fight Slemmer to stop her from running her mouth. On that fateful night of 12 January, Pike, Slemmer, Shipp, and Peterson signed the Job Corps logbook as they were leaving for an outing Slemmer believed was to smoke marijuana en route to a video store so that Pike and she could try to work out their problems.

When the group entered a tunnel at the edge of Tyson Park, Slemmer likely felt that something was not quite right and proceeded to ask Pike where they were going and whether there was, in fact, any marijuana. These questions irritated Pike who began the brutal assault shortly thereafter after they had gone deeply enough into the woods so that nobody could hear them that led to Slemmer's murder.

Pike confessed to initially slamming Slemmer's head into her knee and then throwing her to the ground where Pike continually punched, kicked, and slammed Slemmer's head into the concrete, screaming, "the bi*ch won't die" and that she wanted "to see [Slemmer's] brains flow." According to witnesses Shipp and Peterson, as Slemmer continued to plead with Pike to stop, Pike got angrier and more brutal. Slemmer offered to return to her Florida home, leave her belongings at the Job Corps center, and not tell anyone what happened; however, Pike became more enraged and yelled at Slemmer to be quiet because "it was harder to hurt someone who was talking to you."

In addition to the savage beating, Slemmer had been cut innumerable times with a box cutter and a mini meat cleaver (that Pike had allegedly borrowed from another Job Corps student) to her torso, arms, face, and back including having had her throat slit six times prior to the fatal blow that resulted from having her head crushed by a piece of asphalt. There was also a pentagram carved into Slemmer's chest; however, Pike asserted that Shipp had done that. Pike also confessed to "just watching Slemmer bleed" when the victim got up and tried to run away. Pike admitted to cutting Slemmer's back: "the big long cut."

After the murder, Pike stated that she and Shipp washed their hands and shoes in a nearby mud puddle to conceal the blood, dumped the box cutter, and Pike returned the meat cleaver to the person from which she borrowed it. This person has never been identified.

The physical evidence and co-defendant testimony suggested that the assault and murder lasted from 30 minutes to an hour and consisted of Slemmer repeatedly trying to get up and run away but was prevented from doing so by the co-defendants who also, as Pike testified, contributed to the physical assault by throwing rocks at Slemmer's head and holding her down so she couldn't run away. Later, Pike would testify that she heard voices in her head overriding Slemmer's continual screaming, telling her that she needed to prevent Slemmer from filing charges against her for attempted murder. Pike also admitted that at one point she thought she had heard a noise and went to investigate it to ensure that they were alone, as well as alleging that during the assault she heard Slemmer breathing in blood and jerking but did not let this assuage her anger as Pike continued her savagery.

Even more troublesome, a police video recorded after Pike's confession shows Pike smiling and providing extensive details about the crime at the crime scene, oftentimes mimicking her actions that evening. Many have said that her demeanor on the recording was eerily similar to that of a little girl who was excited and happy that she had experienced the best day of her life and had no problem talking about the events that transpired, the heinousness of her actions, and how she felt about it all.

The facts of the homicide are not nor have they ever been in dispute, thanks to an abundance of evidence. Pike's confession, and witness testimony at the trial.

Pre-Trial Examination

Prior to her trial, Pike was given a battery of assessment tests and examined by numerous psychiatrists including clinical psychologist Dr. Eric Engum who found her to be extremely bright as evidenced by an I.Q. of 111—in the 77th percentile of the general population—which he believed to be remarkable given her difficult childhood and lack of formal schooling beyond the ninth grade. Dr. Engum also found that Pike had excellent reasoning, problem solving, language, and analytic skills, and was also quite adept at paying attention, sustaining concentration, and sequencing information. Dr. Engum concluded that Pike was legally sane and had no brain damage which has frequently been demonstrated to cause violent behavior in some individuals.

Of particular interest was that Pike was found to be marijuana- and inhalant-dependent and also diagnosed with borderline personality disorder. Whereas there are some similarities between borderline personality disorder and antisocial personality disorder such as impulsivity, irritability, aggression, and a self-image that fluctuates between self-aggrandizement and despair, there are several differences. Individuals with borderline personality disorder differ from those with antisocial behavior in that the former—which primarily affects females—is characterized by a lack of remorse, self-destructiveness, black-and-white thinking, alcohol and/or drug use or abuse, unstable relationships characterized by fear of abandonment and extreme swings between love and hate, difficulty in achieving academic and vocational goals, and are more likely to have been sexually abused; while the latter—which affects disproportionately more males—is characterized by a lack of affect and remorse, emptiness, and an ultimate goal of self-preservation.

Pike demonstrated all of the aforementioned characteristics of borderline personality disorder which makes it easier—but not justifiably so—to comprehend how her intense jealousy of Slemmer and fear of losing Shipp made her commit her atrocious acts. In addition to her fear of abandonment, Pike also abused drugs, was likely sexually abused, had contentious relationships, and displayed zero remorse. Dr. Engum surmised that Pike did not act with premeditation or deliberation in Slemmer's murder but, instead, in a manner that was consistent with borderline personality disorder. More simply, Pike had lost control. However, on cross-examination Dr. Engum admitted that Pike's deliberate luring of Slemmer, that she carved a pentagram in the victim's chest, that she brought weapons with her, and that she bashed Slemmer's head into the concrete does, in fact, constitute deliberateness.

That Pike was overjoyed and singing in Iloilo's room describing the murder while dancing around with the portion of Slemmer's skull Pike had taken as a trophy further supported Dr. Engum's diagnosis of borderline personality disorder because she had eliminated who she perceived was in competition for her boyfriend, Shipp, and, therefore, could continue her relationship with him. When questioned about the piece of skull Pike had taken, Dr. Engum said that Pike had no identity and her actions of taking and displaying the skull was a way to get recognition, no matter how misleading and distorted said recognition might be. In fact, after her conviction and sentencing Pike wrote a letter to Shipp which was intercepted by jail personnel that stated that even though she tried to be "nice" to Slemmer by bashing in her head instead of letting her bleed to death she was still sentenced to "fry."

The Trial

There was an abundance of evidence presented at the trial. Physical evidence consisted of crime scene photographs, autopsy reports, bloody clothing, and the piece of Slemmer's skull Pike had taken as a trophy. With respect to this skull piece, Dr. Elkins presented Slemmer's decapitated skull that was reconstructed by Dr. Marks to explain the victim's injuries. The skull presented at trial was complete except for a portion that was missing on the left side of Slemmer's skull. Dr. Elkins demonstrated that the piece of skull found in Pike's jacket fit perfectly into this spot, much to the chagrin of Slemmer's mother who, in a taped interview, stated that Pike was oftentimes giggling and passing notes to her mother and defense attorney during the trial, not unlike an immature middle-schooler.

At the trial, the State introduced photographs taken of Pike and Shipp at the Knoxville Police Department in which both were wearing pentagram necklaces similar to the shape carved into Slemmer's chest. It was presented that both Pike and Shipp dabbled in devil worshiping and other forms of the occult and that Slemmer was a sacrifice for the next day, Friday the 13th. Despite the presence of some type of satanic elements in Slemmer's murder, Dr. William Bernet, Vanderbilt University's psychiatric hospital medical director, testified that the evidence was that of "an adolescent dabbling in Satanism." He further concluded that the concept of collective aggression—or mob mentality—in which a group of people become stimulated and subsequently engage in some type of violent behavior was most assuredly at play in the events leading to Slemmer's death. However, Dr. Bernet ultimately stated that he did not have enough evidence to definitively surmise whether Pike had acted with premeditation or intent when she lured and murdered Slemmer.

Pike was ultimately convicted of first-degree murder and conspiracy to commit first-degree murder after a mere two-and-a-half hours of jury deliberation. The fact that the jury returned guilty verdicts for first-degree murder—and did it so quickly—demonstrate that jurors were convinced that Pike had the requisite mens rea, or mental capacity, to warrant a first-degree murder charge: premeditation and deliberation. Amidst the overwhelming evidence and utter lack of remorse for her actions Pike was sentenced to death by electrocution (Tennessee has since adopted lethal injection for executions but has the prerogative to utilize electrocution if the lethal injection drugs cannot be obtained). Shipp was sentenced to life without parole because his age at the time of the murder was too young to warrant capital punishment and Peterson turned informant and was given six years' probation for her testimony.

Pike's conviction was upheld by the Court of Criminal Appeals and the United States Supreme Court denied certiorari.

Post-Conviction

While incarcerated, Pike demonstrated more evidence of her depravity. In 2001 she tried to murder fellow inmate Patricia Jones by strangling her with a shoelace. Pike alleges that Jones repeatedly tortured her by calling her "fried chicken" and making various demeaning sounds as an affront to what Jones said was the sound that Pike would make when she was electrocuted. The final straw was when Jones physically threatened Pike's friend, fellow devil worshiper Natasha Cornet. Pike said that she jumped atop Jones and choked her with a shoelace so that the much larger and heavier Jones would get off of Cornet. By the time prison guards reached them, Jones was unconscious.

Pike was subsequently convicted of attempted murder despite her prior death sentence because any offense committed while an individual is incarcerated must be adjudicated. During this time, neurology specialist Dr. Jonathan Henry Pincus began investigating Pike's brain to glean some type of knowledge as to why Pike behaved and continued to act violently the way she did when she assaulted Jones. He asserted that every killer he has ever examined share three commonalities: brain damage, a history of abuse, and mental illness. Dr. Pincus alleged that Pike did, in fact, possess all three features and demonstrates all of the requisite features common to serial killers. There is much consensus among professionals that Pike would likely have been a serial killer had she not been caught the first time.

He also testified at Pike's attempted murder trial that her brain's frontal lobes are not "put together properly"; largely due, he claimed, to the fact that Pike's mother drank while she was pregnant with Pike despite denial of this by Pike's mother. It was also brought up that as a child Pike played at the slaughterhouse where her grandfather worked and that she was frequently subjected to pornography and horror movies on the home television screen. He asserted that all of these factors provide insight into how an 18-year old girl could act with such depravity as was the case when Pike murdered Slemmer. However, the original trial judge, Mary Beth Leibowitz, stated that Pincus' "findings" of brain damage was curious as the defense expert at Pike's original trial who was trying to spare her the death penalty failed to find such evidence.

Forensic psychiatrist William Kenner testified that Pike had suffered from undiagnosed bipolar disorder, the symptoms of which were evident from the time Pike was a "sleepless, talkative adolescent" and likened her to an automobile with cruise control set at 120 miles per hour. Pike's post-conviction defense team alleged that this non-diagnosis justified her requesting a new trial.

In 2002 Pike sought to have her appeal legally stopped and to proceed with her execution. In June of that year Judge Leibowitz granted Pike's request and scheduled an execution date of 19 August 2002. However, a few days later Pike changed her mind and the Tennessee Court of Appeals subsequently stayed her execution. In October 2005, Pike's death sentence was affirmed; however, no execution date has been set at this time.

Pike was again in court in 2007 when her defense team headed by Donald E. Dawson asserted sought a new trial, alleging ineffective assistance of counsel in that her trial defense team failed to introduce evidence supporting Pike's alleged bipolar disorder. During this hearing, Shipp admitted to misinforming investigators and that he, in fact, was primarily responsible for Slemmer's murder. He stated that he was drunk and tired and just wanted the police to leave him alone when he put the onus of blame on Pike. Additional testimony from prior Job Corps student and the defendants' mutual friend Tyrone Comfort stated that Shipp controlled and abused Pike despite her assertions that he was the first male to protect her and she admired the respect and fear he elicited from others. Pike, however, was heavily medicated during this hearing for her alleged bipolar condition and the hearing was rescheduled for April 2008.

During her 2008 hearing, prosecutors portrayed Pike as a cold-blooded vicious killer who not only planned Slemmer's murder but prolonged it for sport, essentially playing cat-and-mouse with Slemmer by allowing her to get up and try to escape and then pushing her back on the ground for additional torture. Ultimately, her request for a new trial was denied.

Pike became newsworthy again in 2012 when she formulated an escape plan with the help of 34-year-old New Jersey resident Donald Kohut who frequently visited Pike in prison but the extent of their relationship remains unknown, and 23-year-old former prison guard Justin Heflin. In a joint investigation by the Tennessee Department of Corrections, the Tennessee Bureau of Investigation, and the New Jersey State Police after receiving information about the plan, both men were arrested and charged with bribery and conspiracy to commit escape, with Heflin charged with an additional facilitation to commit escape charge due to his job as a prison guard. Authorities discovered contraband evidence in the facility which could have only been brought in by a staff member and that Heflin was likely involved. Further investigation demonstrated that Heflin knew Kohut and that Heflin was receiving gifts and money for his assistance in the escape plan. Pike was also charged.

Even more recently, during yet another post-conviction relief hearing in 2015, testimony revealed that Pike was allegedly pregnant at the time of the murder. While this may be true it neither excuses her actions nor provides any potential evidence of legal insanity to justify an affirmative defense of not guilty by reason of mental disease or defect or guilty but mentally ill. Also during this hearing, Slemmer's mother requested the missing piece of her daughter's skull so she could bury the whole of her daughter but was denied as the skull piece remains a critical piece of evidence in Pike's ongoing legal appeals.

Since exhausting the state appeal process, Pike's new defense attorney, Assistant Federal Defender Stephen A. Ferrell, filed a 123-page petition on her behalf alleging that he constitutional rights were violated in both the original 1996 trial and penalty phase and that Tennessee's appellate courts ignored said violations. Among these claims is that capital punishment would amount to cruel and unusual punishment in violation of the Eighth Amendment of the United States Constitution because of Pike's youth, immaturity and mental illness. While Shipp—only 17 at the time of the murder—was too young to warrant imposition of a death sentence, Pike was not. Ferrell alleged that her trial lawyers were incompetent and failed to introduce evidence of mental illness, brain injury, and post-traumatic stress disorder. In response, the state Attorney General submitted a 90-page rebuttal repeatedly asserting that the state courts' ruling were all legally correct. As of the beginning of 2016, this battle continues.

Numerous video interviews of Pike over the past several years show her admitting that she was fully cognizant of her actions and that they were wrong. She stated that she felt as though she was taking out years of abuse on Slemmer and that she committed a horrible atrocity and deserves to be punished; however, she asserts that she deserves life without the possibility of parole for her actions; not the death penalty for the actions of three individuals. She has repeatedly stated that she wishes it was she who died and not Slemmer but such protestations are moot after the fact. One cannot help but wonder if Pike actually means what she says or is simply saying what she thinks others want to her. Knoxville Police Department detective Randy York who worked the case has said that in his lengthy career he has not encountered many people who he believes are evil but that Pike is, indeed, the personification of evil and that she should never be permitted to be around other human beings ever again.

Experts assert that the death penalty is not an effective general deterrent and debate over the morality and legality of capital punishment remains contentious and in the forefront of public discourse and debate. Currently, Tennessee is only one of 38 states which have the death penalty. Whereas women comprise 13% of those arrested for murder, only 2% are sentenced to death and, of those, only 3% are actually executed; primarily due to judges not wanting to sentence women to death. In Tennessee, only two individuals on death row have been executed—both males. The last time a woman was executed in the state was in 1837. Many currently believe that Pike will likely never be executed.

SHE DEVIL: THE TRUE STORY OF MYRA HINDLEY

ELLEN THOMAS

In the early 1960s, Myra Hindley took her first job out of school at a small chemical company called Millwards Merchandise. A shy eighteen-year-old, she kept to herself, reading in the office courtyard during breaks.

But she only did this to attract her co-worker, Ian Brady.

Brady would spend his breaks reading books. Myra soon followed suit in the hopes that he would approach.

After several months, the Glasgow, Scotland native finally made his move.

They both worked at the office as clerks. Brady was four years older than her as they began to date.

Myra lived with her grandmother and gave her virginity to the awkward co-worker on her grandmother's sofa. She would soon become Brady's accomplice in some of the most gruesome child killings in the history of Great Britain.

A BAD NEWS CHARACTER

Brady already had a police record for petty theft. He also had a strange demeanor, tilting his head oddly at people as he stared them down with hooded eyes.

He was nicknamed "Lassie", not a reference to the Collie dog but to his feminine body language. Brady was tall, skinny and would indicate later that he was a bisexual. As a child, he had few friends and was called "Dracula" in the neighborhood. He would torture kittens and see how long it took for them to die.

They were both bookworms and Brady would give Myra books on the Marquis De Sade, trying to introduce her to the world of sexual sadism. After their dates, he would invite her back to his place and play back recordings of Adolph Hitler's speeches.

The young couple would come up with pet nicknames for each other. Myra would call Ian "Hetty" after a character in the Goons and he would call her "Hess" after Hitler's deputy. They would soon become inseparable, both strangely odd people that felt that were superior and set apart from everyone else.

It soon became clear, however, that Ian was influencing Myra and not the other way around. He was her guide to the world of sexual sadism and then later, slowly revealed his desire to rape and murder children.

He started this by sharing a book in the same way he introduced her to sadomasochism. The book had detailed the "crime of the century". A child was the victim and one of the characters was named Myra.

"He had given me a book called 'Compulsion,'" Myra recalled. "Which was the story of Leopold and Loeb. They decided to commit the perfect murder. They were studying the philosophy of Nietzsche, his theory of the superiority of the pure Aryan and the strong overcoming the weak. It was very much the Nazi philosophy. They kidnapped a twelve-year-old boy for a ransom. They killed him, were caught and sent to prison. I told him it was a very disturbing book. But why exactly had he wanted me to read it? He told me he wanted to do a perfect murder and I was going to help him. That was why he needed me to pick someone up as I was a woman and a child would be more trusting of a woman. I burst into tears and he slapped my head backward and forward. I managed to fight him off and told him to stop it."

Myra fell prey to Ian's system of push and pull psychology. He would be abusive to Myra then inexplicably turn around and be sweet to her.

"I must be totally honest and say he wasn't always cruel and sadistic towards me," Myra said. "We had some pleasant times in country places that he'd found during his travels on his bike. We'd pack a picnic lunch, lots of coffee, bottles of wine and spend whole days in peace and tranquility. That was such a contrast to the other side of him. These were moments I treasured and thought about when things were bad. Trying to remember, telling myself that he couldn't help what he was and maybe in time he would become accustomed to ordinary domesticity and we could live a normal life."

IDLE HANDS

"Myra was a bored English girl looking for some adventure," forensic psychologist Paula Orange said. "Brady had an edge about him. Myra liked that about him, she wanted out of her dull life and into a world of edgy darkness, if you will."

Myra didn't judge Brady for being an avowed Nazi. She thought he was just going through a phase but he continued to play Richard Wagner's music full blast and storm around the house dressed up in Nazi regalia. Working himself up into a frenzy, he would then play rough sex games with Myra.

Myra found this aspect of Brady's personality to be alluring. She enjoyed dressing up in leather and black stockings, indulging whatever fantasy Brady could come up with.

"She was a sheltered young woman," Orange said. "And Brady opened up a whole new world to her. Think of it as 'Fifty Shades of Grey' with some Nazism thrown in and you have the whole relationship of Myra Hindley and Ian Brady."

The kinky sex continued and Brady gave stronger indications that he wanted to commit the perfect murder.

He wanted to harm children.

But he needed an accomplice.

"We can make the case that Myra made the jump from sadomasochistic sex to murder out of an obligation to Ian," Orange said. "It gave her a rush, to follow his lead. She needed more and more to get that same high."

The two would feed off each other sexually after which Ian would begin to plot the murders out. Who would be their victim? How would they kill them? Where would they kill them? He wrote things out in advance to the most minute detail.

"She (Myra) became desperate to fulfill his fantasies, his needs," journalist Clint Entwhistle said. "She was frightened, I suspect, of rejection by him."

So Myra didn't report him. She went along with his program.

SNAPPED

Brady had made his decision that they were going to kill someone. The night before, he took Myra to a bar on the back of his motorcycle. The two parked a little beyond the pub itself. Ian then began to intimidate Myra. He was jealous that she took a ride home from a co-worker.

"All the time we were talking," Myra recalled. "He was running a knife across his fingers. I honestly thought he was going to stab me. Then he laughed, put the knife away, told me never to accept a lift (the co-worker) again, and we drove back to the pub."

"Later as we were driving home, I dreaded what he would do when we got there, for I knew he would do something. "He raped me anally, urinated inside me and, whilst doing so, began strangling me until I nearly passed out. Then he bit me on the cheekbone, just below my right eye, until my face began to bleed. I tried to fight him off strangling me and biting me, but the more I did, the more the pressure increased. Before he left, when he'd seen the state of my face, he told me to stay off work the next day ..."

This would all take place under the roof of Myra's grandmother who was asleep when the assault took place.

"My gran almost fainted when she saw me and went to get my mother, who asked me if ' He' had done that to me. My mother disliked him intensely and kept telling me he was no good for me; she'd been telling me that since I'd met him at 18 and a half, but what girl of that age listens to her mother when she is wholly infatuated and in love? I told them what he had told me to say (she had been hit by a beer bottle during a bar fight) but I knew they didn't believe me."

THE FIRST MURDER

The following night after he beat down Myra, Brady selected his first victim.

He spotted a teenage girl walking to a dance by herself. She wore a sky blue jacket over a button-down red polka dot dress. Her white gloves and high heels turned on Ian Brady but what really arrested his attention was her face.

Cute with an air of innocence. A face that had an easy vulnerability, someone who would crack under the pressure of his whip.

Her pain and tears would be delicious, Ian thought.

Her name was Pauline Reede.

Brady gave Ian her orders and told her to pick the girl up. He would follow them on his bike.

"Ian Brady was awkward," Entwistle said. "He was not the kind of person a child would trust. There is no way anyone would have gotten into a car with him."

That is what he needed Myra for.

Myra did as he said, driving up alongside Pauline as she walked on the deserted road. The two young woman had already known each other from around the neighborhood.

"Can I give you a lift?" Myra asked.

"Oh, thank you, sure," Polly got into the small white van.

"Where are you going?"

"To the dance hall-"

"Okay," Myra said. "I just have to go to the Moors. I just lost one of my gloves. You can help me look for it. It will only take a second."

Pauline simply nodded her head. She trusted Myra.

THE KILLING FIELDS

"The Moors above Manchester were a special place for Ian Brady and Myra Hindley," Entwistle said. "They picnicked there together. They'd have sex there. It was a very, very important place to them."

It would also be the place where they would commit their first murder together.

Myra stepped off the van and directed Polly to look through some bushes. It was dark and Pauline asked if they should just look for it in the morning. Myra laughed it off and walked away, feigning as if she were looking for her gloves.

Ian Brady waited in the bushes, his mouth dry with anticipation, as he watched the sixteen-year-old Polly sift through the bushes.

Sneaking behind his victim, he slammed her across the head with a shovel.

Pauline Reede fell to the ground, stunned.

She would then be raped, tortured then murdered by the sadistic Brady.

"Brady was a sadist," Orange said. "He got off on the suffering of his young victim. The more innocent she was, the more she screamed, the more she pleaded for her life, the more he got off. It was part of the high for him. He had moved beyond the bedroom thrills with Myra and needed a bigger high. He wanted his fantasy to become reality."

Brady assaulted Pauline until she lost consciousness.

No longer able to provide him the "fun" of listening to her suffer, he took a knife to her throat and killed her.

Myra watched in silence as Ian Brady commit the brutal crime and then proceeded to bury Polly in a shallow grave.

"He led me to her body which I tried not to look at," Myra wrote. "I didn't know at the time that he was testing me at there was no need for me to be there. He told me to look at here. I'll never be able to forget what I saw. I stood and looked at the dark outline of the rocks against the horizon of the dark sky. Three people died that night. Pauline. My soul. And God. No God would have let what had happened, happen."

On the surface, however, Myra didn't seem distressed about the murder. She went to work the following Monday as if nothing happened.

"You would think if she had any conscience left she would have gone to the authorities," Orange said. "But Myra had been dehumanized by that point. The daily rapes and assaults made her numb to everything."

Still, a part of her old self remained. The disappearance of Pauline Reade sent shockwaves throughout Manchester. Myra was reading the newspaper one day and noticed a personal column written by Pauline Reade's mother.

It read " Pauline, please come home. We're heartbroken for you."

"I began to cry," Myra recalled. "Rocking myself back and forth with the paper clutched to my chest. I didn't hear his bike, nor knew that he'd come into the house. He asked me what was wrong but I couldn't answer; I couldn't stop shaking and crying, for I was devastated about what had happened to Pauline, and for her mum and dad. I really liked Mrs. Reade and used to feel sorry for her because she had problems with her nerves and always looked as though she was on the edge of a breakdown. He grabbed the paper off me and soon saw what I'd seen."

"He put the bolt on the front door in case gran came back, did the same to the back door, and began to strangle me. Before I lost consciousness, I heard him remind me of what he'd said after Pauline's murder, and that threat still stood. After the first murder, as we were driving home, he told me that if I'd shown any signs of backing out, I would have finished up in the same grave as Pauline."

MYRA'S EARLY LIFE

As one would expect, Myra grew up in an abusive home.

Her parents engaged in daily shouting matches which she watched from behind her bedroom door.

Her father would routinely beat her mother, exposing Myra to sudden violence during her formative years. He was a competitive boxer who would also engage in weekend bar brawls.

"He used to beat her a lot," Entwhistle said. "Her father was a very, very powerful influence on her life. She had a tough personality type to start with. If you combine that with a violent childhood, a childhood where she was taught how to be violent, how to be aggressive, then you end up with an unusual personality type."

Myra hated her father and saw him as a bully. He would teach her to box, often hitting her across the head when she performed the techniques incorrectly.

"My father wielded total parental control," Myra said. "I rebelled against it. Fought against it. All my life until I was old enough to free myself from it. All his attempts to control me, even the successful ones were at great cost and were the result of bitter recriminations and often a hard physical punishment."

Myra's father would give her spankings without warning, leaving her buttocks bruised.

Once when she was bullied by a little boy and came home with bruises on her face, her father locked her out of the house. He told her to either face down the bully or he was going to beat her up himself.

"I set up the street to meet my persecutor," Myra recalled. "I quickly concentrated on whatDad had told me and showed me. As Kenny's hand came up, I shot up my left hand, fist bunched towards his head. As I predicted, both hands went up to protect his face and I lifted my right hand and slammed it into his tummy, hitting him hard. With a gasp, Kenny Holden's knees crumbled and before he could recover I slammed my left fist into the side of his head. Kenny was so heavily shocked he sat down heavily on the floor and burst into tears. I stood looking down at him triumphantly."

Myra saw a lot of her father in Ian Brady. Aggressive. Ultra-violent.

"Myra did what we call in psychology, 'transference,'" Orange said. "She saw in Ian what she saw in her father. She never got her daddy's love. So in her mind, she saw Ian as Daddy. She wanted Daddy's love and would do whatever Ian wanted. That was part of her cycle. Transferring a deep need for her father's love onto Ian. There is the strong possibility that had Myra never hooked up with Ian she would have never become a murderer. But the two of them together? Horrific results."

"The bringing together of Myra Hindley and Ian Brady," Entwhistle said. "Unleashed an appalling set of criminal acts."

POLLY IS STILL MISSING

The disappearance of Polly Reede sent the town of Manchester on edge. Things like that simply didn't happen there.

"The fact that children were being abducted and killed," Entwhistle said. "Was incomprehensible to the ordinary man and woman in the street."

Myra would soon find out that Ian's sexual fantasies were not limited to teenaged girls.

He wanted boys too.

Myra would again be a willing accomplice in procuring Ian's second victim. This time, it would be twelve-year-old John Killbride. Myra would befriend the young boy before bringing him to the Moors where he would be sexually assaulted by Brady and later killed.

"I had a terrible feeling something had happened to him," John Killbridge's mother recalled when her son didn't come home from school. "Because he wasn't the kind of boy who would leave home for any reason. He was quite happy and very pleasant, always singing and whistling and I just couldn't see him going anywhere with anyone. Unless it was in an innocent way, somebody wanting to do a job with him or something like that. He'd be enticed into a car that way."

Ian would take photos of the body and burial site. This would become part of their ritual, their ceremony. They would perform the murder then take photographs as if to mark the moment. Then they would return to the scene of the crime days after with their dog "Puppet" in tow. They would take more pictures and relive what took place only days earlier.

"He stopped me as I was walking (to take a picture)," Myra recalled. "And said to turnaround. Moved me about a bit. Told me to kneel down and look at 'Puppet' whose head was showing when he was still wrapped inside my coat. I now know, and knew quite soon afterward, that he photographed me virtually kneeling on John Killbride's grave."

AN INSATIABLE HUNGER

Four months had elapsed between the Pauline and John Killbride murders. But now Ian could not wait long. He ordered Myra to deliver another victim to the isolated Moors.

His name was Keith Bennett. An exuberant, trusting boy, Keith looked like the proverbial nerd with a gap-toothed smile and professorial eyeglasses.

"Keith was a cheeky little lad," Entwhistle said. "He liked to go out and have fun."

Trusting that Myra was taking him some place fun, the young Keith was ambushed by Brady who wrapped a cord around his neck.

Myra did her usual best to remain detached while the horrific attack took place.

"I hadn't wanted this to happen," Myra recalled. "I was tense and terrified. I tried to concentrate my mind miles away from where I was. Finally, after roughly what I think was a half an hour by which time dusk began to descend. I heard him whistle or call. When I stood up, he was waving me back down to the stream bed. Virtually nothing was said as we made our way back except for him saying the spade was hampering him and he'd have to hide it, which he did."

The twelve-year-old Keith, whose entire family was waiting for him at his grandmother's house, never showed up.

His entire family would be traumatized for life.

"I am a mother," Keith's mother, Winnie Johnson said. "It was my first lad and I've got to find him no matter what."

Keith Bennett's body was never found.

"I have nightmares," Johnson said. "I jump in my sleep. It's getting to me now. Because I just can't get him back."

Meanwhile, Myra and Ian would once again take mementos of their time together, taking photos of themselves along the Moors on Keith's fresh grave. Days later, the two would go to St. James Church for midnight mass.

"I retained a warm religious glow," Myra said. "And came out feeling warmed. Not so Ian who took a long swill of whiskey and went to the grave where he casually urinated."

RITUALS

The photos of their time together became an obsession for Ian Brady. He had an automatic camera where he would set the timer and pose for photographs with Myra. In a few of them, they would pose on top of the fresh graves with Ian playfully choking Myra.

"Myra and Ian would often return to the scenes of their crimes," Orange said. "They would take photos of themselves there and relive the thrill of committing the murders."

Over time, however, the photos would not be enough stimulation. They needed something better. Something more visceral.

Sounds.

Ian Brady decided he would record the audio of their next victim being tortured.

That next victim would be ten-year-old Leslie Ann Downey. Myra would befriend and abduct her from the county fairgrounds.

"They would take her back to their home," Entwistle said. "Where he photographed her and recorded her being tortured."

Ian Brady would listen to the audio tape over and over again, closing his eyes and remembering the horrific acts he committed.

Is is the murder of Leslie that Myra would refuse to talk about in interviews.

"There's a tape that isn't what people think it is," Myra said, trying to downplay her own sadism evident in the tapes. "But it's bad. I just hurt so much to think that I've been such a cruel bastard."

THE RUSH OF KILLING

Like a drug addict needing a bigger hit to get high, Brady needed more and more of a thrill for his next murder. He started to get sloppy whereas before his attacks were meticulously planned out.

His next victim would be Edward Evans.

"Edwards was sixteen, seventeen years old," Entwhistle said. "And he picked him up in a pub in Manchester."

This would be the first time Ian acted in tandem with Myra to obtain the victim. They enticed the young man to come over to their home and there were witnesses in the pub.

The couple also invited Myra's brother in law, Dave Smith to watch the carnage.

"Smith had no idea what was going on," Entwhistle said. "He walked into it totally cold, totally unaware and soon found out that he was involved in the most horrific scene with blood all over the place. A man's head being smashed in."

Smith was appalled, then called the police and told them of the killing.

Police arrived on scene within minutes. They discovered the mauled body of Edwards in a tub. Both Ian and Myra would be arrested.

"It is inexplicable as to why the couple would allow Dave Smith to witness the murder," Orange said. "A part of me thinks that it was part of increasing the thrill. The desire to share what they felt was a special moment with someone else."

A CHILLING DISCOVERY

Investigators would then scour the home, finding one unusual clue that would reveal the goings on of the couple now known in the papers as the Moors Murderers.

They found a left over luggage ticket.

The police would go to the central train station and matched the ticket with a suitcase. Inside, the found something they would never forget.

"They kept trophies in suitcases," Entwhistle said. "In there, of course, was the tape recording of Leslie Ann Downey and that proved what they'd done."

The police would play back the tapes. It churned their stomach to hear the tearful cries of Leslie Ann Downey plead for her life.

"You need to do what he says," Hindley screamed at the little girl. "I told you to shut your face!"

"I want to go home," the little girl pleaded.

"Quiet! Do you not speak English?"

The tape would be played for the jurors at the trial of the couple.

According to witnesses, you could hear a pin drop when they played the tape in court.

"Afterward there was a long, stony silence," Entwhistle said. "As people reflected on what they just heard."

DENIAL

Myra would maintain her own innocence of the murders and repeatedly state that she never witnessed any of the killings herself.

"My solicitor (defense attorney) told me they'd found the body of a child," Myra said. "Identified as Lesley Ann Downey, did I know anything about it? And I said 'No.' A week after that, I'm not sure, they found John Killbride's body and they charged me with, I think it was the murder of John Killbride. Yes, it was.They set me down behind a table and behind it was a large poster of John Killbride. 'Will you just identify these pictures or these photos and tell us if you seen them before.' I'd say, yes, and then they turned over the picture to another photo of the unearthed body of John Killbride."

The picture, Myra would state, made her cry.

LETTERS TO MOMMA

Myra would write her mother numerous letters before her trial. She would order her mother to destroy the letters after she read them but her mother thought otherwise. She would also tell her mother to keep the photographs of her and Ian to herself.

"Don't believe what they're saying about us," Myra wrote. "It is all lies."

But the mothers of all the victims didn't see it that way.

In court, they all had an opportunity to confront Myra.

"The worst part was being confronted by Mrs. West in the witness box," Myra recalled. "And I was looking at her as she was giving evidence and she saw me looking at her and she screamed across at me. 'How can you look at me?' And she called me every name under the sun."

It is at this point that Myra stated that she began to fully realize the gravity of her crimes.

"It suddenly hit me just what I'd done and I think he (Ian) sensed this," Myra said. "We were sitting next to each other and he just put his hand on my arm and squeezed my arm. And I turned around and looked at him, and he was telling me with his eyes to keep quiet."

The jury would find them guilty and in May of 1966 both would be sentenced to life in prison.

STANDING BY HER MAN

Myra refused to testify against Ian. There were some legal experts at the time who believed that if she gave evidence against Brady she would have walked free. But she didn't. She elected to take the punishment along with him.

Instead, she accepted her sentencing and continued to write her mother.

"Dear Mum," Myra wrote. "I knew that I would have to go to prison for some time for 'harboring'. But I didn't think it would be for this long. Ian is in prison, in the special wing. Poor thing, he sews mailbags during the day. He says it helps to pass the time quicker than expected. Will you do one thing for me, ma'am? Take out a policy on me or for me, for a half gram a week. I can't even begin to think of the future. It will be something to fall back on."

"Ian has got a little mouse in his cell. He feeds it crumbs and sits in bed watching it nibble them. The other night, he left it half a chip, thinking it wouldn't touch it but when he woke up the next morning it had disappeared."

Over the next three years, Myra would bombard her mother with requests for the photographs of her and Ian together. She said she did this at the behest of Ian who wanted both the slides and photographs desperately. Myra's mother eventually relented by was sure to allow the police copies of the negatives.

"Ian wanted those pictures back so bad because it reminded him of the events," Orange said. "That is the sort of thing we've come to expect from certain types of serial killers. They want to relive the moment in their fantasy. They'll take mementos, pictures, different elements of their crime in order so they can relive it in their minds. The pictures of Myra holding their dog on those burial sites were of paramount importance to Ian."

Myra would die in prison in 2002 of respiratory failure. Her ashes would be scattered over the Moors, a place that she loved so much.

"Was Myra Hindley sick or was she evil?" Entwhistle asked. "She had a violent father. She met a sexually sadistic man who desperately wanted to be a serial killer. All those things came together and made her carry out some evil, appalling crimes."

Ian Brady remains alive, living out his years under suicide watch in a psychiatric facility where he has repeatedly stated that he will kill himself if given the chance.

SHE MATES, SHE KILLS: THE TRUE STORY OF TAUSHA MORTON

ALISON YALE

94

AN AGGRESSIVE FLIRT

Dewayne Barrentine met Tausha Morton in early 2007.

She worked as a teacher's assistant at his son's daycare. A single parent, Barrentine would pick up his son and would be greeted by Tausha on a daily basis.

"Whenever I would pick him up," Barrentine said. "She would always make sure to step out into the hallway and give him a hug and say 'hey' to me. She made herself very noticeable."

Tausha gave Barrentine all of the hints that she was interested. The sideways glance, the smile that lingered just a little too long. But still, he needed extra coaxing.

"One of her co-workers actually approached me," Barrentine recalled when a woman in the hallway had passed him a note.

"She said, 'It's a phone number,' I said, 'To who?' She said 'Miss Tausha and she wants you go give her a call tonight. And it started from there."

Smitten by the forward nature of the sweet-faced single mother, Barrentine fell hard.

The two began dating and began living together within a month.

"She was really there for my son...," Barrentine recalled. "I had full custody of him. He would lay in the bed next to me ... and I would hear him say his prayers and he would pray for a mama." He would soon feel the same way about Tausha's daughter, Lexie.

"We weren't dating even a month and she said, 'Will you be my daddy?' And I said, 'Baby, I'll be whatever you want me to be...'"

From that moment, Barrentine became hooked as Tausha made him feel as if she really loved him. She did all the little things from kind words to love letters.

He soon began to realize, however, that Tausha had a manipulative, lying nature.

The tall tales began to pile up. She told Barrentine that she had a "Bachelor's degree in Criminal Justice" as well as an inheritance due to her from an inhertiance.

"It was from her granddad who was a federal judge who was blinded by a battery blowing up in his face. If he was a federal judge, surely his name would be on docs under Google somewhere, but I never found anything."

Barrentine grew increasingly suspicious with Tausha's stories. He did some online investigating and discovered that she had a previous marriage with a man named Mitch Kemp. He confronted her about it and she would state that she had been married five times before.

The two vaguely resembled each other, big Southern boys, "teddy bears" that were more than a little overweight.

After eight months of co-habitation, Barrentine caught Tausha cheating on him.

He promptly threw her out of his home.

"I called the Sheriff's department," Barrentine recalled. "I was like, 'look, I don't care what y'all do with her, she's got to get her shit and get outta my house.'"

Wanting retribution of some sort, Barrentine accessed Tausha's MySpace account as he knew her password.

"Dewayne gets on her Myspace account basically to mess with her," prosecutor Richard Hicks said.

After sifting through her e-mails, Barrentine would make a shocking discovery.

"I found two or three e-mails," Barrentine said. "And they were from Mitch Kemp's sister-in-law."

Mischele Kemp had written Tausha an e-mail with the subject "We're really concerned."

"How is Mitch doing? We haven't heard from you in over our year? We would like to hear from you. If we don't hear from you immediately we will contact law enforcement and media. It is not like Mitch to disappear for years on end without contacting his mother and we have became extremely concerned. Please contact us. We are very worried about him and your entire family. Sincerely, MK."

Digging a little deeper, Barrentine looked into Tausha's "sent message" box and it did not appear that she had ever responded.

"Immediately, I changed the password on the account," Barrentine said. "To where she couldn't access it and I printed off all those e-mails."

His actions would prove to be something bigger than a missing persons case. He would bring all of this information to the local police chief in Florida who instructed him to keep things to himself as he sorted things out with the Boone County Sheriff's Department in Missouri.

WHO WAS TAUSHA MORTON?

Tausha Morton, AKA Tausha Fields, met Mitch Kemp in 2001 when she lived in Colombia, Missouri.

Mitch worked as a carpet installer and had been recently divorced after fourteen years of marriage.

"It wasn't long after he got divorced that he met Tausha," Mitch's brother Rick said. "I would say within months."

Despite their eleven year age difference, Kemp fell hard for the young and vivacious Tausha.

Tausha was the proverbial "people person." Most of her friends and neighbors described her as someone who would make you welcome and treat you as if you were a long lost friend.

"She was bubbly," said one of Tausha's former employers. "Friendly and inquisitive. She paid attention and asked lots of questions about you."

Tausha liked learning about other people. She, in turn, would be all too willing to share details of her own struggles.

"She told us how her whole family was killed in a car accident," Rick Kemp said.

Tausha had a way of getting people to feel sorry for her. She would come across as a heavily burdened individual who suffered a lot of tragedy. People listening to her story would feel compassion for her lot in life and do what they could to help her.

Mitch Kemp listened intently to Tausha's tales of woe, buying them hook, line and sinker. He wanted to help her. To be her rescuer, her knight in shining armor.

The two began to date and by September of 2002, Tausha gave birth to a baby girl.

Mitch loved kids and was ecstatic. He proposed marriage and Tausha accepted.

"They got married in Pensacola," Rick said. "It was a very easy wedding."

The marriage seemed to look okay from all observers. Mitch's family didn't have any misgivings about Tausha, her charm enabling her to get into their good graces, at least at first.

"She was a really sweet girl," Carole Kemp said, recalling her first meeting with Tausha.

But over time, his family began to notice a personality change in Mitch. Sister Mischelle stated that he wasn't "as playful as he used to be."

Family gatherings would "take a back seat to things that she wanted to do" according to Tracy Kemp, who blamed Tausha's ability to manipulate.

As work responsibilities increased for Mitch, things began to go south in their marriage very fast.

DOMESTIC LIFE AIN'T FOR ME

Bored that she was left alone with the baby, the high-strung Tausha needed an outlet.

She would arrive at her friend's gym, the Body Zone, with her baby in tow. Soon she began working part time at the fitness center.

It was there that she would meet Greg Morton.

Morton was more physically fit than Kemp but he fit the same profile psychologically. He had recently broken up with a longtime girlfriend and was be vulnerable to the manipulative charms of Tausha.

"Greg was despondent over his break-up," a family friend said. "But when he met Tausha, he kinda perked back up."

Tausha used the same seductive strategy on Morton as she used on Kemp. She detailed her tragic back story. She told him stories of being molested, of being raped.

She also told Morton in no uncertain terms that her marriage with Kemp was on the outs. Making herself look like the victim, she told Morton that Kemp had made her miserable. He was abusive, bothered her constantly and threatened physical harm.

"She told him a bunch of lies," one of Tausha's friends said. "She said she was getting him (Mitch) served, that they were getting divorced."

By February 2004, her allegations of physical abuse would be reported to the police department as Tausha filed assault charges against him.

"She said he abused her," Rick Kemp said. "By assaulting her, or slapping her or something."

Tausha informed police that she and Mitch had gotten into an argument. Then he hauled off and hit her.

Mitch Kemp would plead guilty to the charges and spend over a month in jail. Upon his release, he would be in for another surprise.

Tausha had moved out of the family home and moved in with Greg Morton, taking Lexie with her. Morton had own a farm outside of Colombia, Missouri, a sizable estate that he inherited from his step-father.

A custody battle then ensued between Tausha and Mitch for their daughter. The fight would get uglier by the day with daily phone calls between the two and their attorneys. She would refuse to allow Mitch to see Lexie and used the courts to prevent visitation.

But Mitch Kemp would not give up without a fight.

"If he had to go through the court system to do it, he would do it," Mitch's brother Rick said. "But that he was going to see his daughter."

Tausha would state that their divorce was finalized in August as the custody battle lingered on. She would then marry Greg Morton the same month.

But Morton had no idea what he was getting into and a "triangle" domestic dispute ensued.

Tausha had arranged to meet with Mitch in order to get some personal belongings. She drove in with Greg to the house of Mitch's friend where he was staying. Mitch confronted Tausha on the front porch where he immediately berated her, screaming insults.

Greg was waiting in the car at the time and went to intervene on Tausha's behalf. Mitch became further enraged and hit Greg over the head with a patio chair.

Retreating, Greg and Tausha sprinted back to the car.

Mitch, however, would disappear after that confrontation.

THE DISAPPEARANCE OF MITCH KEMP

It took awhile for Mitch's disappearance to hit home for his family members and friends. He was the type of man whom you would not hear from from awhile but would suddenly show up on the front porch.

He was dutiful about calling his mother Carole and when she didn't hear from him, she began to worry.

"We called the Boone County Sheriff's office," Rick Kemp said. "About two weeks afterward, probably. We told them that Mitch had disappeared."

The Sheriff's department did not think any foul play was involved. They offered assurance to the family that Mitch "probably didn't want to be found."

Boone County detectives came to that conclusion after they found out that Mitch was wanted for stealing some goods from a friend. They believed he disappeared in order to escape from repercussions of his actions.

Meanwhile, Greg and Tausha were living large. In late 2004, Greg put up his farm for sale which surprised both his friends and family. He treasured the land as it was bequeathed to him from his stepfather. Those close to him believed that Tausha had put him up to it.

In February of 2005, the sale of the farm finalized. With a $275,000 payout in hand, he and Tausha left Missouri, telling no one.

The Kemp family continued to believe that Mitch was not missing and that Tausha was involved somehow. They just didn't have any evidence or clues. Just a damn strong suspicion.

"Something had either happened to Mitch that had nothing to do with Tausha," Rick Kemp said. "Or something happened to Mitch and Tausha had something to do with it."

Both the Kemp family and Boone County law enforcement would then find locating Tausha and Greg to be a fruitless exercise. They literally disappeared from the face of the earth, wanting a new life. Leaving no trail behind, Tausha and Greg would move all the way to the Gulf Coast.

Greg, still smitten by Tausha, would get a tattoo of her name on his back as if he were a branded cow. With a new man firmly under her control, Tausha would go on a spending spree which included getting breast implants with Greg's money.

NO SIGN OF MITCH

By February of 2008, the Kemp family still had not heard from Mitch.

"They took a missing persons report," Rick Kemp said. "But the case went cold, quite frankly, because they didn't do anything about it."

But the Kemp family would not give up hope. They continued their search, turning to the Internet to look for any trace of their beloved son and brother.

They would search different social networking sites and court systems to look for any trace of Mitch.

They found nothing for years.

Until Mischelle Kemp found Tausha on MySpace, the social networking account.

"My sister-in-law found an account," Rick Kemp said. "That had Tausha's name and picture on it."

Mischelle immediately sent Tausha an e-mail.

"Tausha didn't respond," Rick Kemp said. "But Dewayne Berrentine did."

REVENGE SEEKING BOYFRIEND TO THE RESCUE

Dewayne Berrentine read through Tausha's e-mails on MySpace and began connecting the dots.

"Her little stories," Berrentine said. "Just because somebody lies to me, that doesn't mean I'm going to call you out on it immediately. I thought that she was coming up with these stories to impress me, maybe?"

Dewayne had discovered that Tausha had gotten around. He received some disturbing information from a man that Tausha had dated after she met Greg and before she met Dewayne.

His name was Keith Jones.

"I was in love with her and anything else didn't matter," Jones recalled. "You couldn't verify anything that she said," he says. "You know, and I mean there were a lot of stories."

Keith and Dewayne exchanged notes and stories about Tausha. They realized that she told them the same outlandish stories. But then Jones told Dewayne a story that he didn't hear before.

He described how Tausha revealed to him that she was involved in the murder of one of her exes.

"She had a few drinks in her," Jones recalled. "She said this guy had raped her and her daughter. And she apparently ... went to where he was and lured him back to her house ... and he walked in the front door. And that's when Greg shot him in the chest."

Both men thought the story was "so far-fetched" and because of the lies they always heard from her, thought nothing of it.

Dewayne did eventually confront Tausha about the allegation and she dismissed it out of hand, saying that her ex-boyfriend would say anything to throw a wrench into her new relationship.

Dewayne would change his mind about things when he opened Mischelle Kemp's e-mail message to Tausha, however. After notifying the authorities, he also wrote Mischelle Kemp back who in turn contacted the authorities in Boone County. The Sheriff's department then reopened the case. After doing some sniffing around, they discovered that Mitch had "fallen off the face of the earth" and had not filed taxes in over four years.

Finally, the Boone County Sheriff department realized that something was wrong.

INVESTIGATING TAUSHA

Detectives decided to start researching the background of Tausha.

They would discover that Tausha's parents were alive contrary to her account that they were both dead. Mitch's mother had spoken to Tausha's father shortly before her soon was to be married.

"She said, 'Mitch, we need to talk,'" recalled Rick Kemp. "You've heard a bunch of stories. Her family wasn't killed in a car wreck. They're alive. They don't want anything to do with Tausha. They say she's nothing but trouble."

Mitch dismissed the notion of his mother. He was totally smitten with Tausha.

Further investigations would reveal that Tausha had been married and divorced twice by the time she met Mitch Kemp. She would go onto have four marriages before she was thirty and the number of men she lived were numerous. Mitch had no idea that Tausha went from one man to the next man to the next. Even if he did, he was so smitten by her early in their relationship that he would have probably ignored the red flags.

Investigators would further discover that her divorce to Kemp was never finalized so she may have married Greg Morton while she was still married to Kemp.

Tracking her movements after she moved from Missouri proved difficult. Tausha and Greg were eventually tracked to Alabama.

The couple lived an indulgent lifestyle, buying luxury homes and cars on the $275,000 sale they profited after selling the farm.

But it didn't take long for them to blow through the money.

Needing more income to support Tausha, Greg would go to Mississippi in the hopes of finding clean-up work after Hurricane Katrina hit. After he left, Tausha saw it as an opportunity to cut him loose.

She had to find someone new.

"While he was gone doing Katrina," Barrentine said. "She was blowing through his money. Then he came home finding another man laying in his bed and he's broke."

Greg would immediately file for divorce.

MEN AND MORE MEN

Cut off from her money supply from Greg, Tausha would find work as an assistant at a day care center. It was there that she would meet Dewayne Barrentine.

She would follow the same modus operandi in her seduction of Barrentine, telling him the sob stories of her life. She described how Greg Morton would abuse her and how she escaped. She gave details on how Greg would try to "jump on her" and that they had "several physical altercations."

Agreeing to let her move in, Dewayne would meet Greg when he was helping Tausha get her belongings out of his house.

The two didn't fight. Instead, they spoke briefly and Greg would later tell Dewayne about how detectives from Missouri were looking to speak with Tausha.

Barrentine would eventually discover Tausha cheating on him and throw her out of his home. She would find a new boyfriend a few days later by the name of Denver Workman.

Workman left his job and his extended family from Florida to Wilmington, Delaware after Tausha begged him to do so. Then she wanted him to move back and Workman refused.

"She would yell, scream and throw things at me because I wasn't leaving," Workman recalled. "She would tell Lexie I was a bad person and to kick me. I bought her a bus ticket to Florida and let her borrow my truck that was still down there. She took the truck, and I never saw her again."

Police would finally catch up to Tausha in Dothan, Alabama and confront her about the disappearance of Mitch Kemp.

During her initial interrogation, Tausha would firmly deny having any contact with Mitch.

"What do you mean what happened to Mitch?" Tausha would ask detectives in bewilderment. "I haven't had any contact with him. None."

The investigators continued to press, however, and Tausha would try to insinuate Greg as having something to do with Mitch's disappearance.

"They had words on the phone," Tausha told detectives. "And then they had, they got in a fist fight one time."

After being threatened with the possibility of being put in jail and leaving her five year old daughter Lexie in the hands of the state, Tausha then placed the blame on Greg.

"Greg killed Mitch," Tausha said. "He told me."

She would then inform detectives that she wasn't there when it happened. She stated that Greg left about 45 minutes later after he had yet another phone conversation with Mitch.

Tausha would claim that she feared for both her and her child's life because of Greg's temper.

She would recall that Greg shot Mitch on the farm. Investigators played along, even paying for her plane ticket to fly from Alabama to Missouri in order to let them know where Greg had buried Mitch. But once she arrived, Tausha seemed confused by the layout of the farm. She could not pinpoint where exactly the body had been buried.

She was then released under her own recognizance back to Alabama while Sheriff deputies proceeded to dig up the farm to no avail. They used ground penetrating radar, cadaver sniffing dogs but came up empty.

WHERE WAS GREG MORTON?

While talks with Tausha revealed some clues, investigators were even more eager to speak with Greg Morton.

After ending his marriage with Tausha, he settled in St. Louis. He was going to school to become an electrician and had a new girlfriend.

He wanted nothing further to do with Tausha. When investigators approached him, Greg immediately invoked his right to an attorney and refused to speak further.

Detectives did not have enough evidence to charge him. But they had Tausha on the run and spoke to her again. This go around, they decided to employ a little psychological manipulation.

"But I tell you what," Detective Dave Wilson said while sitting across from Tausha in the interrogation room. "He (Greg Morton) automatically assumed that you talked to us. Now, we didn't confirm that."

"Why did he think that?" Tausha asked.

"Well, there's only...who knows?"

"But he said he thought he'd talk to you?"

"I'm going to ask you again. Can you take us directly to where that hole was?"

This go around, Tausha said yes. The Boone County Sheriff's department flew her in from Alabama yet again to Greg Morton's farm.

This time, Tausha led investigators straight to where the body was buried.

Mitch Kemp's remains were dug up and his identity was confirmed.

"It didn't surprise us," Rick Kemp said. "But we were all just blown away. I mean, I just didn't want to believe that my brother was gone."

Investigators discovered that Mitch had been shot numerous times and found numerous shell casings in the makeshift grave. They then went to St. Louis and arrested Greg Morton.

"He wasn't surprised when we showed up," Detective Wilson recalled.

Tausha was allowed to return home but investigators had a suspicion that she was more involved than she let on.

A VOW OF SILENCE

Greg strangely refused to rat out Tausha, remaining in prison until he was officially charged.

Tausha moved to Texas, however, and began dating someone new. Investigators would catch up with her again, however, and this time a heated ninety-minute interrogation would ensue.

Their probing questions would force Tausha to change her story about Mitch's murder completely.

"I did not do anything," Tausha said after detectives informed her that she would be charged with first-degree murder. "I helped you in every way I could possibly fucking help you.

"Tausha," Detective Wilson said slowly. "We got people who say, say otherwise, okay."

Tausha then changed her story again, stating that she was present when Greg murdered Mitch.

"I snuck around behind Greg's back and I saw Mitch, okay," Tausha said. "Greg had no idea."

She stated Greg would kill Mitch in a jealous rage after they returned from a hotel for a tryst. They then drove back to the farm and Greg assaulted Mitch before he got out of the car.

"He had a gun in his hands," Tausha said. "It was a black gun. Mitch started walking backwards. I ran inside the house and then I ran back outside. I saw that Mitch was walking backwards, and Greg was walking towards him. And Greg shot him. I didn't kill Mitch. I didn't want Mitch to die."

But the investigators didn't see it that way. They charged her with first-degree murder.

THE TRIAL

In June of 2009, Tausha had been imprisoned for over six months as she awaited trial.

Her bail was set at one million dollars.

Greg Morton then decided it was time to cut a deal. He broke his silence on what really happened the day of Mitch Kemp's murder. He would admit to his involvement in exchange for a more lenient sentence if he testified against Tausha.

In 2010, Tausha's trial began.

The prosecution's argument was that Tausha was the mastermind behind the murder, that even though Greg pulled the trigger it was

Tausha that put the idea in his head. They also believed that Tausha's motive was to have sole custody of their daughter.

The defense would claim that Tausha was innocent and the victim. Her attorney was, in essence, using the same technique that Tausha used on all of her men. They would play on sympathy and hope that the jury would be as charmed by Tausha as all of her men.

GREG MORTON CONFESSES

Morton would take the stand and tell the jury exactly how Tausha manipulated him to kill Mitch.

"She's hysterical," Morton recalled. "She said Mitch raped her."

"What are you feeling, Greg, at this point?" Prosecutor Hicks asked.

"I wanted retribution. Tausha took charge and handed me a gun the net morning. She goes, 'I'm going to get Mitch, and when I get back, you shoot him.'"

"What were you going to do, Greg?"

"I was going to do what she asked me to do."

"They made a plan in that Tausha was going to go in town and pick Mitch up," Rick Kemp said. "And tell him that Greg was out of town."

Mitch arrived at the farm, thinking that it would only be the two of them. But then Greg emerged from the porch.

"I had a gun in my hand," Morton recalled. "I raised it and pointed it at him. I kinda paused I was kinda struggling with it a little bit. And then she started yelling at me to shoot him."

Greg believed that he was committing a protective act. He believed that Mitch was raping Tausha and molesting their six-year-old daughter.

"Then she said 'You got to get something to move him. Get something to move him with." Greg recalled. "Then she said, 'Come on. You should have had this ready.'"

"And you saw that she was still struggling?"

"He was."

"So what did you do?"

"I shot him again."

"Was he struggling anymore?"

"It was over," Morton said. "I used farm equipment to pick up Mitch's body and we buried him in a pit. When we were rolling the dirty on Mitch she said 'Mitch Kemp is a piece of shit and nobody is going to look for him for a long time.'"

The defense would then call a neighbor who testified on Tausha's behalf, stating that she thought she was under Greg's control.

Greg then broke down on the stand and tearfully apologized to Mitch Kemp's family.

Over time, however, he began to realize that Tausha was a cunning liar. As he got to know her better, he realized that he had been duped.

"He'd been played like a fiddle by her," Rick Kemp said. "She did it to every man that she had."

Tausha was not called to the stand by the defense and the jury would find her guilty.

"I think she thought she was going to walk," Rick Kemp said. "She thought she could just get away with lying and manipulating people."

Tausha Morton was sentenced to life in prison without parole but is currently appealing her sentencing.

SCORNED : THE TRUE STORY OF CLARA HARRIS

GERALDINE TATE

Clara and David Harris looked like the perfect couple. They were both successful orthodontists with a growing practice, a luxury mansion, and three beautiful children. After years of marriage, a rift formed between the two in the form of a sexy receptionist named Gail Bridges.

Clara would go onto suspect her husband of having an affair with the beautiful secretary and have her fears confirmed by a private investigator. Her mind filled with rage, Clara would run her cheating husband down with her Mercedes-Benz.

The story would draw national media attention from Fox News to the Oprah Winfrey Show. There were too many salacious details to ignore; marital infidelity, a scorned woman and rumors of lesbianism.

This is the story of what took place in the rich and privileged world of Clara and David Harris.

A MANSION AND A PICKET FENCE

Clara Suarez had earned the American dream. Born in Bogotá, Colombia, she was raised by a widowed mother and studied dentistry in her home country. In the late 1980s, she came to the United States and completed her residency at the University of Texas-Houston Dental Branch.

Earning her way into the affluence of America, she allowed herself one extravagance.

A Mercedes-Benz.

In 1991, she would meet David Harris at the Castle Dental Center where they both were employed as orthodontists. David had graduated second in his class and had a Texas charm about him, peppering his sentences with "golly."

"Golly" was the first word going through his mind when he first laid eyes on the Colombian Beauty Queen (Clara had won a local beauty contest after she finished her studies). David didn't realize that orthodontists looked like Clara Suarez.

The Latin beauty had lush red hair, a mole on her left cheek and a smile that left David weak in the knees.

She was equally smitten by the uber-successful dentist whom she would marry on Valentine's Day of 1992.

They would have their wedding reception at the Nassau Bay Hilton hotel which would be ess than thirty miles away from where David would open his first dental practice, Space Center Orthodontics.

"I found the best," Clara said after marrying David. "I found the one God had reserved for me."

"They were in love," David's daughter Lindsey recalled. "They were in love and they told each other that often."

A BRIGHT FUTURE

Clara would open a satellite office with David and have photographs of them throughout the workplace. The couple would talk twice a day at a minimum and would never hang up without both of them saying "I love you."

In 1998, Clara would give birth to twin boys. David thought she would be a good mother and she had gotten along splendidly with David's daughter from a previous relationship, Lindsey.

His daughter would stay with them during the summers while spending the school year with her mother in Ohio.

Clara made for a dutiful mother to both her own sons and Lindsay as she was always sure to be home on time to cook dinner for the family.

On the surface, she had attained the American Dream. The perfect life in an affluent neighborhood aptly called "Friendswood."

"She really had the perfect life for a long while," one of her co-workers said. "It made us all envious. She had a beautiful family, a loving husband, and a huge house. She had everything a woman could wish for."

There were competing opinions on David, however.

Writer Steven Long described him as a "self-indulgent, egotistical clod. Everything about David was have the best of everything. Have the best looking woman. Have the best car. Have the best house on the block which they did."

But his co-workers saw David differently.

"He didn't have the type of personality that I would describe as a ladies' man," one of the office workers said. "He did wear a toupee, so there was some insecurity there. But he wasn't the kind of guy who would go out and look to have affairs. That is the way some in the media have portrayed him and I didn't see him like that."

Both David and Clara would attend Shadycrest Baptist Church where they would do more than sit in the pews. David would play the drums for a Christian rock band called "The Colemans" while his wife had an earnest believe in Christianity, thanking God for the life she was able to live.

David passed down his love of music to his daughter. They had a $90,000 piano brought into the house where they would share their love of music together with Lindsey herself being a budding violinist.

BUILDING A LIFE

Not everything had always been perfect for David. His previous marriage ended because his first wife thought he was too career-oriented. The allegation was probably true, David had built his own practice and was in the process of buying out other dental practices in the area. He would hire out his own management team who then outsourced the staff.

His acquisitions mounted and he would see his investments begin to earn dividends. He would earn almost $35,000 a month from his own practice and neared the same amounts with each of the other practices.

David then purchased an enormous office, over 6,000 square feet where he would create the largest orthodontic practice in the region. His entrepreneurial streak saw the future in that he would have a one-stop center for dental work and other orthodontic specialties in one spot. He beamed with pride when his daughter told him that she wanted to become an orthodontist one day. He remarked that he would have an office waiting for her if she decided to pursue that route.

David had it all.

Or he thought he it all until he met Gail Bridges.

THE NEW GIRL IN THE OFFICE

Gail Bridges would join David's practice in 2001 as a receptionist. She was a divorced mother of three; stylishly dressed and petite as she retained the tight body of the high school cheerleader she once was. Remarkably fit at thirty-nine years of age, Gail had youthful porcelain skin, big brown eyes and curves that were artificially enhanced.

"Gail Bridges is a little cutie," Long said. "She's a pretty good looking woman herself. So it was a situation where David just wanted it all."

Gail had previously been married to Steven Bridges, one of the more successful insurance agents in Houston. Like Clara, she had the appearance of having a perfect life. The Bridges had lived in a gated community called South Shore Harbor which was just a freeway hop away from Clara's Friendswood.

Gail spent her days at the local cafe, gossiping and laughing with the other well-to-do housewives of the area.

But her divorce to Steven Bridges left her high and dry as she was forced to find work.

Gail would move out of the gated community and start work at David's Space Center Orthodontics. She would make only $1,800 a month but she enjoyed the job after setting her sights on the head man in charge, Dr. David Harris.

David would normally spend the hours away from treating patients in his back office calling on the other practices and making sure things were okay. But now that Gail Bridges was in his employ he would find excuses to hang out at the front desk and flirt with her. Six months after she was hired, David asked her if she wanted to have lunch with him, making sure everyone was out of earshot.

Gail agreed and two months later they were having an affair.

David and Gail would meet at the Nassau Bay Hilton, the site of his wedding reception less than ten years ago.

"It didn't appear that David was in love with Gail the same way he was in love with his wife," a co-worker said. "He was just obsessed with her looks. Or maybe it was encroaching middle age that made him do what he did. You can't really know. She was really attractive and frankly he couldn't help himself when she arrived to work in her tight skirts and blouses."

Clara was none the wiser at first.

Before Gail's arrival, she would call the office and David would run to the phone in order to talk to his wife. But with Gail on hand, he'd have the other receptionists tell Clara that he would call her back or he would just leave her on hold.

Gail was not well-liked by the other women in the office who thought that her flirting was too brazen.

On one occasion, David had asked for a file that Gail had to bend over and retrieve. Instead of kneeling down, she bent straight over in front of David so he could get a doggy-style view of her ass.

Problem was, Gail did this in front of David's own daughter Lindsey who was in the office.

The rumors of the affair soon progressed from back office gossip to someone feeling that it was necessary to break the news to Clara.

Diana Sherrill was the first to speak out about the inappropriate nature of David's relationship with Gail.

"You could almost feel the chemistry between them," Sherrill said. " ... All the other office workers were nice, but they'd be physically ill by the time they left for the day. They didn't say anything for fear of losing their jobs."

"I thought she was really nice and really pretty," Lindsay said when she first met Gail. "She was petite and bubbly. Her hair was perfectly in place, and her nails were done. I thought nothing of it at first until I saw her put her hand his leg...she was the aggressor."

"The affair became quite obvious to the employees in David's orthodontic office," Long said. "And one of them eventually went to Clara and told her."

After much deliberation in the office, it was decided that Diana Sherrill should be the one to inform Clara of David's affair.

"I told her she needed to protect her marriage," Sherrill said. "Not to ignore anything out of the ordinary, maybe go to counseling to get help. Sometimes men go through a change of life, and maybe that's what was happening to David."

Clara was frightened by the allegation. Could it be true? Then she went into denial and thought that Sherrill had made the story up to destroy her marriage.

But one night after David came home late, she confronted him.

"Where have you been?" Clara asked.

"Out with my friends," David said.

"A girlfriend?"

"What?"

"Are you seeing Gail?"

"Yes," David said after a long and guilty pause. "But nothing happened. I haven't done anything. I kissed her hand."

"You kissed her hand?"

"Look," David pleaded. "I'll do anything to save our marriage. Anything."

"Fine," Clara said. "You fire her tomorrow. We go to marriage counseling. You tell your parents. You tell our pastor."

Clara then went to tell Lindsay about what her father had been doing.

"There's something you need to know about your Dad," Clara said.

"I know already," Lindsay stopped her. "All the girls in the office know. They go out for lunch every day."

With Lindsay being more forthcoming about her father's activities than he was himself, Clara knew her worst fears were true.

"The news of the affair simply crushed Clara Harris," forensic psychologist Paula Orange said. "She had put everything into her marriage. She owed everything she had to David. Her house, her standing in the community, her business colleagues. People in the office knew before she did! She was now socially shamed. She could not cope with all that."

Instead of taking her anger out on David, however, Clara wanted to know anything and everything about her rival.

Clara demanded to know what David saw in her. What was it about her that would make him cheat and destroy everything they had?

David refused to reveal his thoughts until Clara pestered him. Then he let loose, giving specific details on how Clara didn't measure up to his sexy receptionist.

"She has a boob job," David taunted. "You don't. She doesn't have an ounce of fat on her. She has an amazing body. She communicates well. You don't. She's perfect! She's smaller than you and fits better in bed with me than you. Sex with her is a fantasy come true. We have sex three times a day."

"That is the kind of man David was," Orange said. "He was not satisfied with telling Clara that he was cheating on her. He had to give her a laundry list of details as to why Gail was better than her in every way, beauty, personality and in the bedroom. He crushed her heart than stomped on it."

A BROKEN WOMAN

Clara took David's words to heart. She thought that if she got into better shape, if she was more affectionate with him in the bedroom then the dentist would see the light.

"If she had sex with him three times a day, " Clara recalled. "I would double that. I would hire a personal trainer, get a membership at a tanning salon and had my hair and nails done every day. Then I put a deposit down at the plastic surgeon's office for a boob job and some liposuction. Then I hit the mall and got some sexy outfits."

"Clara went on a rigorous exercise program and lost weight," Orange said. "She thought that by getting in better shape that her rival that David would cease the affair. She didn't understand the psychology behind David's behavior at all, instead, she concentrated on her own perceived shortcomings and didn't realize that no matter what she did her actions would do nothing more than drive him further into her arms."

Clara made a resolution to devote herself entirely to David. She called the office and retired from her dental practice. She informed them that she would dedicate herself to her family.

David, on the surface, appeared remorseful. He had sat down with both Clara, daughter Lindsay, and his own parents to confess about the affair.

He asked for their forgiveness.

David did not want to break off all communication with Gail, however. He told his family that he wanted to meet her one last time at a restaurant and tell her that he was sorry.

He wanted to take all blame for the affair and tell Gail that it was not her fault.

Clara did not agree to this stipulation at first but eventually relented when David assured her that he would meet with Gail at a public place.

"David said one thing to Clara and his family," Orange said. "And another to Gail. He would appear remorseful with Clara and probably did have feelings of regret for hurting her. But when he was with Gail he would change his tune. He would tell her that she was his one true love and that his marriage with Clara was just one of convenience."

Clara would sense the ambivalence going on in David's heart. Her husband had asked for forgiveness but would later let his guard down and reveal that he was missing Gail.

She decided to call a private investigator named Bobbi Bacha to follow her husband and make sure that he was, in fact, staying away from Gail.

A LEOPARD DOESN'T CHANGE ITS SPOTS

"She said 'here's all the information'," Bacha said when Clara entered her office. "'He's going to meet her tonight. If you could get close and get recordings of what they're saying."

Bacha would have a member of her team follow David. Clara decided that she would follow David as well to make sure the meeting took place at a restaurant. She had Lindsay come along both as moral support and as a witness.

"She was kind of nervous about it. She had doubts," Lindsey said, of Clara. "She kept doing her hair and kept going shopping. She was nervous."

Clara got a call from the detective agency who told her that they had lost the couple while they were following them. Clara decided to take matters into her own hands and drive to places where they thought they would be. They stopped off at a popular steak restaurant, a cafe, an aquarium and then Gail's house.

They didn't find the couple.

Then the detective called Clara back.

"They are at the hotel," the private investigator said. "On the fourth or fifth floor. Be patient and you will get a full report tomorrow."

The hotel was their normal meeting place for sex.

The Nassau Bay Hilton.

The same place where David had exchanged wedding vows with Clara.

"He went into the hotel room and checked in," Bacha said. "He was with the other woman. And at that point, we just videotaped them coming out. And there's no reason a married man would be in a hotel room with another woman unless there is adultery."

Clara would receive the news and go bonkers. She sped toward the hotel, scaring step-daughter Lindsay who told her to slow down.

Clara wouldn't listen. She told Lindsay to call her father on the phone and inform him that one of the twin boys had taken ill.

"David Harris?" the dentist said, answering his phone in his professional tone of voice.

"Daddy?"

"What is it?"

Lindsay hesitated. She didn't want to be the pawn in between her step-mother and her father. But Clara motioned for Lindsay to continue talking. "You have to come home. Bradley is sick."

"What?"

"Come home, Daddy, please."

"And that is where our story becomes incredibly violent," Long said. "Because she (Clara) saw them come out of the elevator, hand in hand. And Clara Harris lost it. Clara attacks Gail and wrestles her to the ground in the lobby of this hotel."

THE ATTACK

"We were leaving the hotel and I was looking at David and I noticed all of a sudden his face changed," Gail said in an interview with News2Houston. "And I went to look at the direction, and then we saw her. Soon after that, it all turned into massive turmoil, and the only thing that I could do was to yell for help ... for someone to please, please get her off of me."

Clara sprinted toward the couple like an enraged tigress.

"You bitch, he's my husband!"

She slapped Gail then ripped at her shirt. Gail tried to grasp on to Clara's wrists but the scorned woman was too enraged.

"This is Dr. David Harris!" Clara pointed at David with one hand while clawing at Gail with the other. "And he's fucking this woman right here!"

Lindsay herself felt betrayed by her father as well. He had asked her for forgiveness in front of everyone and now here he was, caught red-handed with his mistress once again.

"I hate you!" Lindsay slapped David with her purse. "I hate you! I hate you!"

Meanwhile, Clara had tackled Gail to the ground and began pounding her head into the linoleum. Hotel employees managed to wrest Clara away from Gail but she would not relent. She escaped from the grasp of the men holding her back and attacked Gail again, biting her in the calf.

But there was one last humiliation for Clara as the hotel employees pulled her back off.

"It's over, Clara," David said as he attended to Gail. "You've blown it, it's over."

Clara screamed and attacked again, grabbing Gail's shirt.

David then got physical with his wife, pushing her to the floor before escorting Gail out of the lobby.

Police had not been called as the altercation looked to have ended.

"There was nothing but rage going on in Clara's head at that point," Orange said. "There was no rational thought, no thought of the future. If anyone needed some psychological counseling at that point, it was Clara Harris. She was a woman scorned and someone was going to pay the price. She didn't have a knife. She didn't have a gun. But she did have a car."

Hotel employees would escort Clara and Lindsey back to her Mercedes-Benz. They told them to leave the premises immediately.

Clara had other ideas.

She spotted her husband attending to Gail and her mind raged.

Screaming like a banshee, she floored the gas pedal.

The car screeched ahead toward Gail's Lincoln Navigator.

David pushed Gail out of harm's way as Clara smashed into him.

"That was David," Clara recalled. "He always thought he was such a macho man."

Her Mercedes-Benz side-swiped Gail's SUV then hit David, sending the dentist flying through the air, only to land twenty-five feet away on his back.

"According to my investigator," Bacha said. "His face hit the dash and his teeth went flying everywhere."

"I was just expecting the car to stop right there where you park," Clara recalled. "That concrete little thing—I thought the car was going to stop there, but obviously, it didn't. It just picked up air."

Lindsay screamed. Gail screamed.

Bacha's investigator had videotaped the entire confrontation.

But Clara wasn't done.

She turned the car back around and sped toward Gail.

"No!" her step-daughter screamed.

"I could hear someone yell at me to get away from my car," Gail said. "To get away and I didn't quite understand why until I turned and looked. That was when she struck me on my leg with the vehicle."

She came back around and ran over David again.

And again.

And again.

Gail screamed in horror. Lindsay turned hysterical.

"Every time that car hit him," Long said. "His body was going through a meat grinder."

"You're killing him!" Lindsay screamed.

Clara finally stopped the car and exited the driver side.

"I got out of the car like a zombie," Clara said. "I couldn't believe David was on the floor—I had just seen him running. I couldn't understand why he was just laying down, like nothing."

David laid on the gravel parking lot. Barely breathing, his body remained limp.

"I told him 'look, look what she's done,'" Gail recalled. "His last words to me were, 'I'm sorry, I'm so sorry' and then he lost his life shortly after that."

Clara kneeled down and took David in her arms.

"David," she screamed. "Look at what you made me do!"

Lindsay got out of the car, yelling at Gail.

"She killed my dad. She killed by dad."

THE AFTERMATH

Clara would be sentenced to twenty years in prison. She would later claim that it was impossible for her to have known she had run over David.

"I didn't blame them because everything that they heard in that court, it was horrible," Clara said. "I hated the woman that they were describing. They only heard the prosecution's side. I didn't blame them. In that moment, I don't blame them. They didn't have anything in their hands to do anything else than what they did. They never heard what really happened."

"Clara Harris loved him too much," writer Steven Long said. "She was willing to kill to keep anyone from having him. Unfortunately, it was David who got killed."

Although Clara leaned on David's daughter for support at the time, Lindsay eventually testified against her stepmother during the trial.

"From the day this event occurred," Lindsay wrote. "I've tried to avoid doing anything to commercialize or promote the story of my dad's tragic murder. The person who murdered my dad, unfortunately, has not exercised the same restraint."

"Clara has appeared in print and on television to persuade the viewers that she is actually the victim, but she is no victim. What she did was the ultimate act of selfishness, caring only about obtaining revenge and thinking not one bit about how her horrible act was going to affect me or my brothers, Brian and Bradley. Anyone who shared my ride in the car that evening, seeing my dad's face as he was about to be hit, and experiencing the horrible feel of the car bumping over his body would understand that this murderess deserves no sympathy."

GAIL GOES INTO HIDING

Gail Bridges would go into hiding after the murder and in some ways be the subject of as much media scrutiny as Clara.

"The affair was wrong," Gail said. "I do not regret or will ever regret that I got to know him and that he became part of my life. He once told me that he would like to spend the rest of his life with me, and he did."

Reporters would discover that this would not be the first time that she was accused of having an affair, only the first time she was accused of having an affair with a man. During her divorce trial, Steve Bridges would claim that Gail had been having a lesbian affair with Julia Knight. Knight's husband would make the same claim during his own filing. These are claims that were never proven. Valerie Davenport, the attorney for both Gail and Julia would state the lesbian affair scandal was concocted by both husband's in order to throw dirt on their own trail which included substance abuse by Steve.

But the salaciousness of the allegations was too much for the media to ignore. Gail and Julie had made a previous appearance on the Sally Jesse Raphael show where they talked about their husband's attempts to paint them as lesbians (both Gail and Julie wore disguises). This videotape surfaced during the media circus for the Clara Harris trial and Gail was once again brought under public scrutiny.

OPRAH WINFREY

Clara Harris would later make an appearance on the Oprah Winfrey show where she expressed sadness at her actions.

"It's a terrible tragedy," Clara said. "Something that I don't wish anybody to go through. So many women I would like to talk to about facing a situation like this. You should never be by yourself. You need somebody who can take care of you. Because when you're in a situation like this, you're not responsible for the actions. You cannot tell what you can do. You know, I found myself in a situation that I never thought myself capable of."

Clara Harris remains incarcerated as she was denied parole in a recent hearing.

KILLER OR CHRISTIAN?
The True Story of Karla Faye Tucker

BECCA BENTON

"My change doesn't bring back any of those lives. But society shouldn't want me to stay in a 'killer' frame of mind. That's okay if they say change doesn't matter as far as 'no, she shouldn't get off on death row' or 'yes, she should be executed.' But surely they wouldn't want me to stay in a killer frame of mind. You think? I hope not." - Karla Faye Tucker

"She always said someday she would be famous." - Steven Griffith, Karla's ex-husband.

There are numerous competing stories regarding the life and persona of Karla Faye Tucker. There is one camp that considers her to be one of the vilest killers in modern Texas history. Then there is another camp who believes that she underwent a religious conversion in prison and that her life should have been spared.

Karla Faye Tucker murdered two people in 1983. She would convert to Christianity upon entering prison and a movie was produced that chronicled her life and reformation. Fifteen years after she committed her crime she would be put to death by lethal injection.

Did she really change? Does it even matter?

This is the story of Karla Faye Tucker, one that resonates almost twenty years after her execution.

GOING NOWHERE FAST

"Karla was a problem child," forensic psychologist Paula Orange said. "No one expressed shock at her behavior when she was arrested for murder. It was almost as if they expected her to do something really bad. Karla was on the fast train to hell at an early age."

Karla was the youngest of three sisters, born and raised in Houston, Texas.

The family did have some good times. Sister Kari Ann was one year older than Karla while Kathi Lynn was two. The family had a German Shepherd and took summer vacations in Caney Creek in Texas where her father Larry owned a cottage.

"I was an itty-bitty girl," Karla recalled during a 700 Club interview. "We were family, and we used to go to the bay house and do neat things with the boat and dog and water skiing and fishing and stuff, but it didn't last very long."

Her father worked as a longshoreman while her mother was a secretary. Her mother was quite pretty and her father had a rugged handsomeness. In their photos together, they look to be a loving and good looking couple with the world as their oyster. But their relationship was tumultuous and the couple would begin a long cycle of breaking up then getting back together again. They would finally divorce when Karla was ten. It was during the divorce testimonies that Karla would find out that she had been the product of an extra-marital affair. This explained to Karla why she always felt inferior to her older sisters who were blonde-haired and blue-eyed. Karla was an odd duck with a screechy voice and a large birthmark on her arm.

"I don't know why my parents divorced; I was too young to know," Karla said. "My dad got custody of us girls, and we all wanted to go with Mother...My father couldn't control us real good. He tried to discipline us, but we were just too much, just too much."

Karla was almost always the smallest girl in her class. Early photos showed her to be a tomboyish looking girl with a bright and vivacious smile. But Karla had begun using drugs in elementary school and she never stopped. The highs and lows of her drug addiction led to her already short fuse growing even smaller.

"Karla was a very violent person," homicide detective J.C. Mosier said. "She would fight with you in a minute. A man or a woman. She got into many barroom fights. She was a tough little gal but she never had anywhere to go but prison. She was destined for prison."

"Some people end up being cheerleaders," Karla said. "And end up in that circle. I ended up on the opposite end of the totem pole. I wasn't born a bad person. And I don't always have to be a bad person."

"She had two strikes against her but they were very big," Orange said. "She grew up in direct vicinity to a drug epicenter in Houston. The neighborhood she was in was rife with drug use and it was the thing to do for all of the kids to just fit in. Karla herself would talk often about peer pressure but was careful to not lay responsibility for her behavior on anyone but herself. Her second strike was her own mother who modeled the worst behavior imaginable for all three of her daughters."

A lot of blame has focused on Karla's mother who led her on the path to destruction.

"Her mother was a drug addict and a prostitute," Mosier said. "But she always had a normal, square day job as a secretary."

Karla's mother brought her daughters up with no rules or lines that you couldn't cross. Karla could do whatever she wanted and to hell with anyone who got in her way. For example, Karla didn't learn how to roll up a joint from her ne'er-do-well friends at school or around the neighborhood.

She learned from her own mother.

"She had gotten caught with rolling up a joint in the house," Orange said. "Her mother caught her and instead of chastising her for having drugs in the house she criticized her for not knowing how to properly roll a joint. But being the good mother that she was, she immediately gave Karla instructions on 'how to roll up a doobie.'"

DO AS I SAY EVEN IF IT KILLS YOU

Karla's mother had introduced both her and her sisters to drugs. Karla would follow the lead of all three and hang out with a biker gang in the neighborhood who called themselves the "Banditos." Karla would go to a lot of their parties and would lose her virginity to one of the bikers when she was only twelve years old. The biker had talked her into joining him in a lover's lane spot where they did drugs and he had sex with the underage girl. Karla, however, enjoyed the experience as it made her believe that "sex on high was the ultimate trip."

She had a devil-may-care attitude toward life. Her academic studies were non-existent as she was a constant discipline problem at school.

"Her teachers had given up on her," writer Linda Strom said. "Her mom was living her own life. A party life. Encouraging Karla to go with her into that lifestyle. Karla herself would start smoking marijuana when she was eight. So by the time she was twelve she was shooting heroin."

Karla's father could not fare better with the girls although he tried harder than his ex-wife. Problem was, he would never be home to enforce any discipline. Larry Tucker would work two 16-hour shifts and be absent from the home with the girls got back from school.

"This was a Lord of the Flies scenario if there ever was one," Orange said. "You have three pre-teen girls with no supervision. Absolutely none. Their mother wasn't an adult herself so how the hell could she raise three girls?"

"Karla was doomed from the beginning. Her mother got her into prostitution and coached her in sexual techniques. So when we are discussing her childhood we have to say that it was very, very brief. There was no extended adolescence here. Her mother robbed her of her innocence probably from the day she was born. Karla never had a chance."

At the age of fourteen, Karla began working as a prostitute...at her mother's lead.

"Her mother was her idol," Strom said.

"(My mother) took me to a place where there was all men and wanted to school me in the art of being a call girl," Karla recalled. "I wanted to please my mother so much. I wanted her to be proud of me. So, instead of saying no, I just tried to do what she asked...The thing is, I knew deep down inside that what I was doing was wrong."

Karla's mother was a rock groupie in addition to being a prostitute. In addition to hanging out with the biker gangs, the two would travel with the Eagles, The Marshall Tucker Band, and the Allman Brothers.

AN ATTEMPT AT DOMESTICITY

At the age of sixteen, Karla married a mechanic by the name of Stephen Griffin.

The couple started off well enough. Stephen fell in love with Karla's tomboy ways and her willingness to stand up for both herself and him.

"We fist-fought a lot," Stephen recalled. "I've never had men hit me as hard as she did. Whenever we went into a bar, I didn't have to worry because she had my back covered."

But Stephen soon realized that he had married damaged goods. When they got high, drunk or even had sex it was all well-plowed soil for Karla. She was a wild horse that needed to be set free.

It would not take long for Karla to decide that married life and the prospect of having children was not in the cards for her. She left Stephen and returned to her old ways of hanging out with biker gangs.

"Karla appeared to have tried that straight road for awhile," Orange said. "She had the type of personality that would try just about anything once. Still, Stephen Griffin is lucky he came out of that relationship alive. It was the typical teenage puppy love we are going to be forever type of thing at first. Then he found out that Karla is a whole different kind of sick puppy."

Karla spent her remaining teen years on into her twenties partying it up in the low-rent housing projects of Houston. She did it all and loved it. Booze. Cocaine. Heroin. And lots of sex.

She would eventually meet an older man in Danny Garrett and the two hit it off immediately. Danny didn't judge her for being a prostitute and supplied her with drugs.

"Karla just could not stay away from the whole biker drug scene," Orange said. "It was all she knew. Some kids have parents who are doctors and nurses and they do likewise. Karla was at the opposite end of the spectrum. Her mother was a whore who serviced rock musicians and biker scum. Karla had resigned herself to the same life."

LIGHTING THE FUSE

Karla had become friends with Shawn Dean, one of the "biker mommas" that used to hang out at the same parties. Shawn was deferential and timid while Karla was fiery and aggressive. The two were fire and ice.

Shawn had a boyfriend named Jerry whom Karla took an instant dislike to. She didn't like men with big egos and particularly did not like men who beat on their women, especially if that woman was her best friend.

Jerry was an obnoxious loud mouth. The guy had rolled his motorcycle inside Karla's house one day and dripped oil over the carpet. Karla got pissed, complaining about the exhaust fumes stinking up the house. Karla and Jerry had words and she kicked both he and Shawn out of her home. The two would have altercations a few times after that with one violent episode.

"One time he was sitting in his car outside," Karla recalled. "And I punched him in the eye for just being there."

Jerry Dean was typical Texas biker trash. He had long hair, squinted eyes and the facial expression of someone who was perpetually high.

His beatings on Shawn began to increase an intensity, open palmed slaps soon turned into closed fist punches.

The abuse was both physical and verbal. Karla decided to interject herself on Shawn's behalf on many occasions which led to his increasing dislike of her. There was an instance where someone had found a picture of Karla posing with her mother. Jerry took hold of the picture and slammed a butcher knife through the photo, enraging Karla.

"Jerry and Karla had a bad relationship," prosecuting attorney Joe Magliolo said. "Allegedly he had cut up some pictures of Karla and her mom which really upset Karla to the point where she had actually hit him, broke his glasses and cut his eye."

The feud between Jerry and Karla would come to a head on June 13th, 1983.

A three-day party had taken place in Karla's home where she had lived with Danny aka "The Pill Doctor." The celebration was for Karla's older sister Kari Ann. Karla's sister wanted an orgy of sex and drugs. Karla and Danny provided that and more.

"Who wants dessert?" Danny called out as he entered the living room with a tray of uppers and downers; dilaudids, valium, mandrex, and placydils.

"Woot! Woot!" Karla's sister Kari did cartwheels in the living room.

The party goers wasted no time in getting high while others indulged in both the drugs and sex.

'I had been doing a considerable amount of coke and bathtub speed," Karla recalled. "I didn't usually do speed much; heroin and downers was my preference because I am a very hyper person and doing speed always 'skitzed' me out made me go crazy...(That night) we were cooking speed, and we started shooting it because it was there, and I loved the needle in my arm. I was what one would call a needle freak."

Karla's friend Shawn arrived at the party with a bloodied nose and a busted lip. She had left Jerry a week earlier but he caught up with her again, getting in another beating which she would not report. Karla saw what her arch enemy did to her best friend and went ballistic.

"I saw what he had done to (Shawn), and I was really mad (because) I was really protective of her," Karla Faye said. "I thought, 'Yeah, I'll get even with him!' My idea of getting even with him meant confronting him, standing toe to toe, fist to fist."

Initially, Karla did not plan to kill Jerry. She just wanted to give him the same treatment he had given poor Shawn.

Karla popped pill after pill, the drugs fueling her need for revenge. While other party goers danced and frolicked with hazy brains, Karla stewed. She ordered Shawn, Danny and a friend named Jimmy Leibrant to the kitchen in order to discuss how they were going to get back at Jerry.

"I want to beat the living shit out of him," Karla slammed her palm on the kitchen counter.

"Damn, take it easy girl," Danny said.

"Take it easy nothing," Karla grabbed Shawn's face and turned it to Danny. "Does that look like taking it easy?"

"Fine," Danny shrugged his shoulders before swallowing a handful of uppers. "Let's go whip his ass."

"You guys-" Shawn started but stopped when Karla's sister Kari and her boyfriend Ron entered the kitchen. The idle threats soon turned into jokes with each person describing in exaggerated terms just how bad they would kick Jerry's ass.

"These were very immature young people in a drug haze," Orange said. "There was not one rational thinking person in the entire group. They had spent their entire lives chasing the next high and really had no idea of the consequences of their actions simply because there never were any. The answer to Shawn's problem was never to leave and never come back. The answer is to kick Jerry Dean's ass. And they wound up killing him."

Danny left the party that evening for his bartender job. Karla drove him to work and would come back at two o'clock in the morning to pick him up when his shift ended.

After dropping her boyfriend off, Karla returned to her home with most of the party goers now gone. Shawn remained and told Karla her tale of woe over a bottle of tequila. Her vivid descriptions of his abuse only enraging Karla even more.

"Karla really didn't like men very much," Orange said. "She inherited this hatred from her mother. When she set her sights on getting revenge on Jerry Dean he became the sum total of every man that ever done her wrong in life. Karla didn't just have baggage when it came to men. She had a whole freight load of it. And she was going to take it all out on Jerry Dean."

THE ROBBERY

The home invasion started out as a simple burglary. Karla wanted to give Jerry a scare while her boyfriend Danny looked to steal the biker's motorcycle. They both saw that as the ultimate sign of disrespect. Stealing a biker's Harley Davidson.

Karla and Danny were joined by James Leibrant as they drove up to Jerry Dean's apartment at three o'clock in the morning on Monday, June 13th, 1983. Leibrant stayed outside as he went looking for Dean's car. Karla and Denny entered the apartment without breaking in. Karla had the keys to the door, finding them after Shawn said that they were "lost."

The couple entered the bedroom and Karla sat on Dean. Jerry then grabbed onto Karla and the two struggled. Danny pulled them apart, smashing Danny over the head numerous times with a hammer that he found on the floor. He struck Jerry with such force that his head separated from his neck and his breathing passages began to fill with fluid. Danny then ransacked the house, finding the motorcycle parts that he wanted and taking them to his truck.

Meanwhile, Karla grew irritated at the "gurgling sound" coming from Dean and wanted to "stop him from making that noise."

Karla found a pick ax next to Dean's bed, something he was using perhaps as a weapon for home defense.

"Karla started swinging the ax on Jerry," Mosier said. "I think it was an accumulation of booze and drugs and her intense hate for Jerry. Jerry was struck around thirty-five times, as I remember."

What Karla didn't know was that Deborah Thornton was sleeping next to Jerry.

She had tried to remain as quiet as possible but an errant strike of the ax had struck her in the shoulder.

Karla pulled the covers back to reveal Deborah. She hesitated for a moment then her criminal mind kicked in.

Deborah was a witness, she had to be killed.

Karla attacked, grazing Deborah in the shoulder with the ax. Deborah fought back and the two grappled before Danny came into the room and separated the two.

Deborah was in such pain that she begged the duo to just kill her.

"'Just please kill me,'" Orange said. "She didn't plead for her life. She wanted them to get it over with. She was in the wrong place at the wrong time. They were both married to other people. They had just met in a bar and Jerry had taken her home."

Karla was only too happy to oblige as she slammed away with the pick-axe. Blood splattered the air. Later Karla would brag that she had experienced an orgasm with every blow she hit Deborah with.

Danny would egg Karla on. He covered Deborah with a blanket and encouraged Karla to drive the pick-axe into her body.

"Come on!" he screamed. "Pretend it is a piñata."

The last blow struck Deborah in the chest, impaling her.

With that, the couple would grab up as many motorcycle parts as they could and leave the apartment.

"It was a horrible scene of violence," Mosier said. "It left a lot of us, even those who had thought we had seen it all, just amazed at the brutality of the crime."

Karla and Danny were not out to commit the perfect crime and get away with it. Instead, Karla went around bragging about the murder, telling anyone who would listen how she pick-axed the couple to death. She felt that it would add to her reputation as the toughest, craziest bitch in Houston.

"I not only didn't walk around with any guilt," Karla recalled. I was proud of thinking I had finally measured up to the big boys. I didn't care about anybody...I didn't place any value on myself or anybody else."

A co-worker of Dean discovered the bodies the next morning as he was waiting for him to come pick him up. The police were called and it didn't take long for them to establish who some of Dean's known associates were. They would use the testimony of Jimmy Leibrant as state's evidence, allowing the man to walk away as they prosecuted Karla and Danny.

OPEN AND SHUT CASE

The couple would go to the home of Danny's brother after the murder. Doug Garrett knew that the two had done something horrific and decided to secretly record their confession.

"Was both of them people asleep when you all went in there?" the police chief asked.

"Mmm hmmm," Danny said.

"Did you all take that ax over?"

"No," Doug said.

"It was already there?"

"Yeah," Karla said.

This audio recording along with the taped interrogation of the police chief would be enough for the prosecution to ask the courts for the death penalty.

"Did you enjoy the killings?" the police chief asked during Karla's interrogation.

"Hell yes!" she squealed.

The jury would be visibly sickened by Karla's lack of remorse on the audio.

"The tapes were her undoing," Orange said. "The jury was chilled to the bone. Had she shown some remorse, shed a crocodile tear or two then maybe she would have gotten a life sentence in lieu of the death penalty."

CONVERSION OR CON?

It was when she was imprisoned, however, that Karla claimed to have undergone a startling transformation.

She had gotten a hold of a Bible and began reading the book for the first time. Tears streamed down her face as she read page after page.

"As she read the Bible," Strom said. "Something hit her and for the first time realized what she had done. It's a genuine radical story of someone who is in darkness and walks into light."

"I think this was a real conversion," Mosier said. "I really think she became a Christian. A good person. It was a metamorphosis from what she was to what she became. It was really amazing and really true, in my mind, it really happened. She wasn't a phony. I don't think there was a phony bone in her body when she died."

Karla and Danny would be tried separately for the murders but her boyfriend would die of liver disease in 1993.

Karla would enter a plea of not guilty and proclaim to be a born-again Christian after her indictment. She would marry her prison minister, Reverend Dana Lane Brown, in 1995. The two would hold their wedding ceremony on prison grounds.

"The Lord put it in my heart," Brown said. "If you'll walk through the circumstances I'll deliver Karla into your arms. I knew that the Lord had spoke to my heart and we believe it and we're standing on it."

"Everybody loved her," Strom said. "I met officers who said 'my life was never the same after I met her., after I had that encounter with her.' I have to say that too."

Karla would appeal for a retrial numerous times between 1984 and 1992. She stated that she was under the influence of drugs at the time of the killings. Her story had drawn the attention of Pope John Paul II, televangelist Pat Robertson and Ronald Carlson who was the brother of Deborah Thornton.

All of them lobbied for Karla to be removed from death row.

"I'm pro death penalty," Robertson said. "But this is one case where I take an exception. This woman has clearly been transformed. To take her life now would not be a matter of justice. It would be vengeance."

Additionally, the warden of Huntsville prison testified on her behalf and stated that she had likely been reformed.

The husband of Deborah Thornton remained unconvinced of Karla's conversion. Despite his own wife cheating on him with Jerry Dean, he refused to believe in Karla's religious transformation.

"Gender politics and grandstanding played a key role in some of her apologists coming out," Orange said. "Religious leaders like the Pope and Pat Robertson refused to believe that women could be capable of such evil. A sweet-faced woman like Karla Faye Tucker was simply led astray like Mary Magdalene in their minds. All she needed was a little Jesus and she would turn out all right. You can contrast their position on Karla with their silence on Danny Garrett who was persona non grata."

Karla would write the following letter to the Texas Board of Paroles and Governor George W. Bush.

"I am in no way attempting to minimize the brutality of my crime. It obviously was very, very horrible and I do take full responsibility for what happened...I also know that justice and law demand my life for the two innocent lives I brutally murdered that night. If my execution is the only thing, the final act that can fulfill the demand for restitution for justice, then I accept that...I will pay the price for what I did in any way our law demands it...It was...three months after I had been locked up, when a ministry came to the jail and I went to the services, that night accepting Jesus into my heart. When I did this, the full and overwhelming weight and reality of what I had done hit me...I began crying that night for the first time in many years, and to this day, tears are part of my life...Fourteen years ago, I was part of the problem. Now I am part of the solution. I have purposed to do right for the last 14 years, not because I am in prison, but because my God demands this of me. I know right from wrong and I must do right...I don't really understand the guidelines for commutation of death sentences, but I can promise you this: If you commute my sentence to life, I will continue for the rest of my life in this earth to reach out to others to make a positive difference in their lives.

I see people in here in the prison where I am who are here for horrible crimes...I can reach out to these girls and try to help them change before they walk out of this place and hurt someone else."I am seeking you to commute my sentence and allow me to pay society back by helping others. I can't bring back the lives I took. But I can, if I am allowed, help save lives. That is the only real restitution I can give."

Governor Bush would not be impressed. Publicly, Bush described the pending execution as a "concrete in his chest, a decision that was weighing him down." But he would later be interviewed by conservative commentator Tucker Carlson who would describe Bush as having derision toward Karla and her supporters.

"I watched [Larry King's] interview with [Tucker], though," Bush said. "He asked her real difficult questions, like `What would you say to Governor Bush?' "

"What was her answer?" Carlson asked.

"`Please,' Bush said going into a whiny impersonation of Karla. "`Don't kill me.' "

THE FINAL DAYS

"I'm not afraid of dying," Karla said before the execution. "I know that Jesus has already begun to prepare a place for me. I know if I have to go February 3rd that he is going to come and escort me personally. So I don't fear that. But I am certainly going to be concerned for those who are going to be left behind. For my family and friends. My husband."

"When she was getting ready to go to her execution," Strom said. "She said to me 'I'm praying that my execution will give those who can't forgive me the freedom to forgive so that they're free of this and don't have to spend their whole life dealing with what I've done."

For her last meal, Karla ordered a banana, a peach and a garden salad with ranch dressing. Karla would invite four people to watch her die; her sister Kari Weeks, husband Dana Brown, friend Jackie Oncken and Deborah Thornton's brother, Ronald Carlson.

"There was never any way out for Karla," Orange said. "From the moment, she was born it was as if she were doomed. Everything came too late for her. Whether her conversion was real or not, ultimately it is inconsequential to the lives of Jerry Dean and Deborah Thornton. They were truly the only ones who could forgive Karla."

On February 3rd, 1998, Karla was executed by lethal injection. As the lethal toxins went through her boy, Karla praised Jesus, licked her lips and looked to the ceiling above. She hummed for a few minutes then went silent. She was pronounced dead eight minutes after the injection.

"I love you, Karla!" her sister wailed.

"Just glowin'," Karla's husband, Rev. Dana Lane Brown said afterward. "The love of Jesus radiatin' through her and around her."

Karla would be buried at Forest Park Lawndale Cemetery in Houston.

"You have to think about others," Karla said in her final words with the 700 Club. "Every choice you make has an effect on somebody else's life. Every decision we make affects somebody else's life. And there are consequences whether they are positive or whether they are negative. We have to get back to the basics of what God says in the family and everything and we need to let our lives be governed by the morals of God by the integrity of God and until we do it is almost an 'I don't care' attitude. It's 'I don't care about others' I just only care about myself. Out there before I knew the Lord I always said I had to look out for number one. Which was me or nobody else would. But we know who number one is don't we? We know that number one is Jesus and number two is others and then us. And if we can really live our lives that way our world would be changed."

www.ingramcontent.com/pod-product-compliance
Lightning Source LLC
Chambersburg PA
CBHW031406150726
47989CB00002B/551